10

MINUTE GUIDE TO

ACCOUNTING FOR NON-ACCOUNTANTS

by Dr. Wayne A. Label, CPA

alpha
books

Macmillan Spectrum/Alpha Books

A Division of Macmillan General Reference
A Simon & Schuster Macmillan Company
1633 Broadway, New York, NY 10019-6785

International Standard Book Number: 0-02-861407-0
Library of Congress Catalog Card Number: 96-078166

00 99 98   8 7 6 5 4 3 2 1

Interpretation of the printing code: the rightmost double-digit number is the year of the book's first printing; the rightmost single-digit number is the number of the book's printing. For example, a printing code of 98-1 shows that this copy of the book was printed during the first printing of the book in 1998.

Printed in the United States of America

Brand Manager: Kathy Nebenhaus
Production Editor: Michael Thomas
Copy Editor: Erik Dafforn
Cover Designer: Dan Armstrong
Designer: Glenn Larsen
Indexer: Chris Barrick
Production Team: Jeanne Clark, Juli Cook, Cynthia Davis-Hubler

CONTENTS

Introduction

What is Accounting? Who needs it? How does it benefit my business? How does it benefit me personally? This book answers these questions for the non-accountant.

Accounting provides information so that you can increase your chance of making correct decisions in your business and personal life. Accounting is the language of business. Like other languages, it has its own terms and rules. Understanding this language and learning to interpret it is your first step to being successful with your own business and personal financial life.

In your personal life you use accounting information to make such decisions as investing in the stock market, applying for a loan, and evaluating potential jobs. Businesses use accounting information for such decisions as planning and budgeting, and borrowing and investing. In general, accounting aids businesses in the process of making better decisions.

Banks use accounting information to make decisions about granting loans. Government agencies base their regulations on accounting information they receive. Many groups have an increased interest in financial statements to determine what impact companies have on their constituents such as environmentalists, labor unions, and local communities.

As the economy becomes more complex, so do the transactions within a business. As these transactions become more complex, so does the process of reporting them to various users. Thus, this book is important to people of all walks of life who have a need to understand this "language of business."

Conventions Used in this Book

This book uses three types of icons to help you quickly find important information:

tip Tip icons offer ideas that help you cut corners and avoid confusion.

 Plain English icons define new terms.

! **Panic Button** icons identify potential problem areas and how to solve them.

DEDICATION

Dedicated to my best friend and wife, Christine. Thanks for your long hours of review and time listening to me talk about accounting.

ABOUT THE AUTHOR

Wayne A. Label is a professor of accounting at the University of Nevada, Las Vegas. He is a CPA and has taught at several universities and has lectured on accounting in several countries. He has written many books and articles on accounting and is a consultant to international companies. He is an expert witness for small and large businesses in the area of accounting systems. In addition to his interest in accounting, Dr. Label is a jazz disk jockey.

INTRODUCING ACCOUNTING AND FINANCIAL STATEMENTS

In this lesson you learn the definition of accounting, who uses accounting information, the different forms of businesses, and the basic financial statements that are used in business today.

WHAT IS ACCOUNTING?

The purpose of accounting is to provide information that you can use to increase your chance of making correct financial decisions. Accountants provide information that helps you produce goods or services as efficiently as possible to maximize profits and keep costs low.

Accounting The process of recording, classifying, and summarizing economic events in a process that leads to the preparation of financial statements. Accounting is the language of business. It provides information to people who want to make sound business decisions.

Accounting is the language of business. Like any other language, accounting has its own terms and rules. To understand how to use this information and how to interpret it, you must first understand this language. Understanding the basic concepts of accounting is essential if you want to be successful in business.

Accountants furnish three types of information:

- Information prepared exclusively by people within the firm (managers, employees, owners)

- Information required by various government agencies

- General information about companies to people outside the firm, such as investors, creditors, and labor unions

WHO USES ACCOUNTING INFORMATION?

All decision-makers need different kinds of information to make their decisions. The more complex the decision, the more accurate the information must be. In the world of business, accounting plays an important role in these various decision-making processes.

Who are these individuals and groups that use accounting? They are as diverse as business itself. They include anyone or any group that plans to interact with a particular business.

Individuals like you use accounting information all the time to make such decisions as:

- Investing in the stock market

- Applying for a loan to purchase a home

- Evaluating potential jobs

- Whether to make, buy, or rent various goods

Managers within a business use accounting information daily to make marketing, production, sales, research and development, and other decisions. Without the proper accounting information these types of decisions would become very difficult, if not impossible, to make.

Banks use accounting information to make decisions about granting loans to individuals and companies. The loan process cannot even begin without the proper accounting information being submitted by a company or an individual.

Government agencies, such as the Internal Revenue Service (IRS), the Securities and Exchange Commission (SEC), the Federal Trade Commission (FTC), the Bureau of Alcohol, Tobacco and Firearms (ATF), and so on, base their regulation enforcement and compliance on the accounting information they receive.

Not-for-profit organizations use accounting information just as profit-oriented businesses do. This information is used in the areas of budgeting, payroll, and reporting to outside entities.

Recently, many groups in the community have had an increased interest in businesses' financial statements. Groups such as environmentalists have attempted to determine what impact companies are having on the environment. Labor groups are interested in the impact that management's financial decisions have on their unions and other employees. Local communities are interested in the impact that decisions made by large businesses will have on their citizens, such as decisions about layoffs or plant closings.

As the economy becomes more complex, so do the transactions within a business. As these transactions become more complex, so does the process of reporting them to various users, and making them understandable for their decision-making process.

FINANCIAL STATEMENTS

Accountants supply information to people outside the firm by issuing formal reports called *financial statements*.

 Financial Statements Reports prepared by companies and individuals on their financial status.

The financial statements are usually issued at least once a year. In many cases they are issued quarterly or more often where necessary. A set of rules, called *Generally Accepted Accounting Principles*, governs the preparation of financial statements. Generally Accepted Accounting Principles (GAAP) has been defined as a set of objectives, conventions, and principles to govern the preparation and presentation of financial statements.

The principal financial statements include the Balance Sheet, the Income Statement, the Statement of Retained Earnings, and the Statement of Cash Flows.

The financial statements for various types of businesses vary in form depending upon the type of business that has been formed. In general, three types of business forms exist in the United States: proprietorships, partnerships, and corporations.

TYPES OF BUSINESSES

Proprietorships are businesses with a single owner. In general, these types of businesses tend to be small retail businesses. The accounting for these proprietorships includes *only* the records of the business—not the personal financial records of the proprietor of the business.

> **!** **Keep Them Separate** The financial records of an individual owner should not be combined with those of the business.

Partnerships are very similar to proprietorships, except that instead of one owner, there are two or more owners. In general, most of these businesses are small to medium size. However, there are some exceptions, such as with large accounting or law firms that may have more than 2,000 partners. As with proprietorships, accounting treats these organizations' records as separate and distinct from those of the individual partners.

Corporations are businesses that are owned by one or more stockholders. These individuals may or may not have a managerial interest in the company.

> **!** **Will You Manage?** Owners in proprietorships and partnerships usually have managerial roles, whereas in corporations they usually do not.

Stockholders are owners of the company because they have purchased shares, whether it is one share or thousands. The stockholders may or may not have a vote in the company's long-term planning, depending on the type of stock they have purchased. However, simply by being stockholders (owners), they do not have decision-making authority in day-to-day decisions. As with the other two types of business organizations discussed here, the accounting records of the corporation are maintained separately from those of the individual stockholders.

In this lesson you learned what accounting is, what businesses use accounting, and about the basic financial statements used in these businesses. In Lesson 2 you learn about one type of financial statement—the Balance Sheet.

THE BALANCE SHEET

In this lesson you learn about the first of four financial statements, the Balance Sheet. You learn about the components of the Balance Sheet and how numbers are attached to each of these components.

WHAT IS A BALANCE SHEET?

Imagine that you make a list of everything that is valuable to you. Along with this list you attach values to all of these items. Then you make a list of everything that you owe to others, and again you attach values to these items. Then you subtract the total value of the second list from the total value of the first. At this point you have the basic components of a Balance Sheet.

 Balance Sheet   A listing of the assets (items owned), liabilities (items owed), and owner's equity (what belongs to the owner).

Your first list can be described as or labeled Assets. *Assets* are valuable resources owned by the business. These items have future value to the organization and can be either short- or long-term.

Asset   Something of value that is owned by the company.

Your second list can be described as or labeled Liabilities. *Liabilities* are obligations to pay others for resources that were furnished to the business. The parties to whom the company owes money are normally called *creditors*. The creditors have a claim against the assets (not a particular one, but the assets in general). The liabilities can result from the purchase of items (Accounts Payable), from services of employees who have not yet been paid (Wages Payable), or from the use of utilities for which payment has not been made (Utilities Payable).

Liabilities   Debts of the business. They can be either short-term or long-term, depending upon when they become due.

Your third list, the one resulting from subtracting the second list of items from the first list, can be labeled Owner's Equity. *Owner's equity* reflects the amount the owner has invested in the firm. There are two sources of owner's equity:

- The amount provided directly by investors, called *Owner's Investment*

- The amount retained from profits, called *Retained Earnings*

Owner's Equity   The difference between what is owned and what is owed. This residual belongs to the owners.

At this point, let's look at the Balance Sheet for Christine's Bicycle Shoppe. A single individual owns this company. (The Balance Sheet looks a little different for a partnership and a corporation. Both of these types of businesses' financial statements are discussed in future lessons.)

CHRISTINE'S BICYCLE SHOPPE
BALANCE SHEET
DECEMBER 31, 1998

ASSETS

Cash	$17,385
Inventory	13,000
Prepaid Insurance	1,000
Accounts Receivable	9,000
Land	10,000
Building	25,000
Truck	8,000
Total Assets	$83,385

LIABILITIES AND OWNER'S EQUITY	
Liabilities:	
Accounts Payable	$3,000
Mortgage Payable	20,000
Total Liabilities	$23,000
Owner's Equity:	
Owner's Investment	50,000
Retained Earnings	10,385
Total Liabilities and Owner's Equity	$83,385

By looking at the Bicycle Shoppe's Balance Sheet, you can see that the bicycle shop has several items, or assets, that belong to the company and are valued at $83,385. You can also see that the bicycle shop has several obligations to pay others, or liabilities, valued at $23,000. Finally, when you subtract the liabilities from the assets (list two from list one) you can see that the bicycle shop has a value after paying its obligations of $60,385. This represents the amount of money that Christine has invested into her business, and the profit that was earned and retained in the business during 1998.

WHAT DOES THE DATE ON THE BALANCE SHEET MEAN?

There is a great deal of disagreement as to how accountants arrive at the values shown on the Balance Sheet. Of most concern are the values attached to the assets, and consequently to the owner's equity, or, as some call it, the *net worth* of the business. The Balance Sheet represents a statement of financial

WHAT IS HISTORICAL COST?

As you saw earlier, all of the items on the Balance Sheet have numbers attached to them, but where did these numbers come from? In the United States, accountants and other users of financial statements have agreed that all values used on all financial statements (including balance sheets) are based on historical cost.

Historical Cost   The amount paid for an item by the business, or the amount incurred in a debt (on the date of the agreement to enter into the obligation).

Therefore, the values on the Balance Sheet for the Bicycle Shoppe do not represent what the assets or the liabilities are worth today if they were to be sold or liquidated. Instead, the values represent what was paid for the assets and what the business agreed to pay to the creditors on the date of the obligation.

Know Your History   Do not assume that the Balance Sheet represents the value of the business in today's dollars. The only asset that can be said to represent its value both today and historically is cash. Since the historical cost convention has been agreed upon in the United States (it has not been agreed upon in all other countries of the world), the Balance Sheet represents only the historical values of these items.

position at a particular point in time. This statement represents a "snapshot" of the business on a specific date. In the case of Christine's Bicycle Shoppe, this point in time is December 31, 1998.

> **!**
>
> **One Fine Day**   The numbers represented on the Bicycle Shoppe's Balance Sheet represent the financial position of the business *only* at this exact point in time—not December 30, 1998, not January 1, 1999, and not any other point in time except the date for which the Balance Sheet was prepared.

THE ACCOUNTING EQUATION

Often the relationships between assets, liabilities, and owner's equity are shown in terms of a formula:

$$A = L + OE$$

The formula depicts the relationships of the various elements of the Balance Sheet. Balance Sheets are often set up with the assets on one side (the left side) and the liabilities and owner's equity on the other (the right side). Thus, this formula shows the same relationships in a formula format.

The same formula can be stated in the following format:

$$A - L = OE$$

In stating the relationship in this manner, you can immediately see what you saw with the preceding two lists. If you subtract the second list (liabilities) from your first list (assets), you are left with the owner's equity of the business.

Does this confuse the reader of the financial statements? No; because everyone has agreed to follow this convention, everyone preparing and using these financial statements understands the language being spoken.

In this lesson you learned what appears on the Balance Sheet and why historical numbers are attached to it. In Lesson 3 you examine the components of the Balance Sheet.

A CLOSER LOOK AT THE BALANCE SHEET COMPONENTS

In this lesson you learn about the components of the Balance Sheet in greater detail. You also learn the interrelationship among these components.

A revised Balance Sheet for Christine's Bicycle Shoppe from the one shown in Lesson 2, with the proper subheadings commonly used in accounting, would look like the one shown here.

CHRISTINE'S BICYCLE SHOPPE
BALANCE SHEET
DECEMBER 31, 1998
ASSETS

SHORT-TERM ASSETS

Cash	$17,385
Inventory	13,000
Accounts Receivable	9,000
Prepaid Insurance	1,000
Total Short-term Assets	$40,385

LONG-TERM ASSETS	
Land	$10,000
Building	25,000
Truck	8,000
Total Long-term Assets	43,000
Total Assets	$83,385

LIABILITIES AND OWNER'S EQUITY

SHORT-TERM LIABILITIES	
Accounts Payable	$3,000
Current Portion of Mortgage	1,000
Total Short-term Liabilities	$4,000

LONG-TERM LIABILITIES	
Mortgage Payable	19,000
Total Liabilities	$23,000

OWNER'S EQUITY	
Owner's Investment	$50,000
Retained Earnings	10,385
Total Liabilities and Owner's Equity	$83,385

ASSETS

As was demonstrated in Lesson 2, assets are items of value (historical value) and are owned by the entity for which you are accounting. Let's make this idea more specific. For an asset to be listed on the Balance Sheet of a company, the item must pass three tests.

The first test is that the company must control the item. This usually means that the company owns the item. For this reason, a traditional Balance Sheet does not list the employees of a company because the company does not own these individuals. A question always comes up during this discussion as to basketball players or other professional athletes. Doesn't the team own them? The answer is *no*. What the team owns is not the players themselves, but the players' *contracts*. Therefore, in this situation, the basketball team ownership would list the contracts of the players as an asset.

The second test is that the item must have some value to the company. Almost anything that is used in the business to earn income and to generate cash does have some value. Certain items that meet the first requirement might be eliminated from being listed as assets by this test. Examples might include an old truck that does not work or inventory that cannot be sold any longer because it has been superseded by newer items.

The third test is that the item must have a value that can be measured. An example of an item whose value can be measured would be the old truck just mentioned. The company purchased it for a fixed amount of money and the company has a record of this transaction. However, let's assume that a company has built up a thriving business, and some of the reasons for this growth are the reputation of the owner and the location of the shop. Neither the reputation of the owner nor the location of the shop has been paid for, nor do we have any way of measuring a value to put onto these items. Therefore, they fail the third test and cannot be listed as assets of the business.

To summarize, for an item to be listed on the Balance Sheet of a company it must meet the following three criteria:

- It must be owned by the company.
- It must have some value to the company.
- It must be measurable.

Quick Test: Can you list three items that would not meet one or more of these tests?

Answer: Christine's own bicycle, a broken tool that is not used in the business any longer, and employees; even though they are of value to the business, employees are not listed as assets since their value cannot be measured.

Short-term Assets

Assets are normally subdivided on the Balance Sheet into two categories. The first is called *short-term assets* (or *current assets*). These items will be used or converted into cash within a period of one year or less.

 Short-term Assets   Items that will be converted to cash (or are cash) within a period of one year or less.

Quick Test: Can you give three or more examples of a short-term asset?

Answer: Cash, securities, accounts receivables, and inventory.

LONG-TERM ASSETS

Long-term assets (also called *non-current assets*) are not expected to be converted to cash or totally "used up" for a period of greater than one year. Long-term assets include equipment, land, and buildings.

 Long-term Assets   Items that will be converted to cash after a period of one year.

INTANGIBLE ASSETS

Intangible assets are assets that cannot be physically touched. They still meet the three tests mentioned earlier in order to be listed on the Balance Sheet as an asset; however, they do not have any tangible characteristics.

Quick Test: Can you list examples of intangible assets?

Answer: Trademarks, patents, and copyrights.

 Intangible Assets   Items of value to a company that do not have tangible qualities but meet all the other tests of being an asset.

LIABILITIES

Refer to the Balance Sheet of Christine's Bicycle Shoppe at the beginning of the lesson. The total liabilities of the business are equal to $23,000. As with the assets, the liabilities list represents both short-term and long-term items. Again, similar to the list of assets, the *short-term liabilities* will be paid off in a period not to exceed one year. The *long-term liabilities* will remain as debt to the entity for longer than one year.

With long-term debt, each year a portion of it becomes due and payable. Thus, most companies' Balance Sheets show the current portion of all long-term debt separately, in the short-term section of the liabilities.

OWNER'S EQUITY

As discussed in Lesson 2, the equity of Christine's Bicycle Shoppe comes from two sources. The owner's investment of $40,000 represents the amount invested in the business by Christine. The retained earnings of $10,385 represents the amount of profit earned by the business since its inception, less any money that Christine may have taken out for her personal use.

A very important point about retained earnings often causes confusion among owners of small and large business alike. retained earnings in a business is not equal to cash. Just because a company has kept profits in the business over the years does not mean that all of these profits have been retained in the form of cash. For example, after a company earns a profit, it may take the cash and purchase some assets or pay off some of its liabilities. Because of this confusion, business owners often assume that they are doing well because they are making profits. If they do not have sufficient cash, however, they will find themselves in dire straits because they will not have enough cash to make the payroll, pay their taxes, or pay for other liabilities. It is critical that businesses have a good cash management plan, which is discussed in Lesson 8.

> **"Retained" Doesn't Necessarily Mean
> "Liquid"**   Retained earnings and profits do not
> translate into cash. A company may have large
> profits but insufficient cash to meet its liabilities.

In this lesson you learned the definitions of the components
of a Balance Sheet and how these components relate to each
other. You also learned a very important point: Retained earnings are not necessarily comprised of only cash. Therefore,
cash management is as high a priority to a business as making
a profit. In Lesson 4 you learn about additional transactions
that impact the Balance Sheet.

Transactions that Affect the Balance Sheet

In this lesson you learn how individual transactions affect and change the Balance Sheet.

Lesson 3 presented the Balance Sheet of Christine's Bicycle Shoppe at the end of the year 1998. Referring to this Balance Sheet, let's examine the transactions that created it.

Investment in the Shoppe

First, let's assume that on January 1, 1998, Christine invests $50,000 in her bicycle shop. In other words, she takes $50,000 out of her personal bank account and sets up a new account with the bank for the new business. After this transaction, the shop's Balance Sheet looks like this:

CHRISTINE'S BICYCLE SHOPPE
BALANCE SHEET
JANUARY 1, 1998

ASSETS		LIABILITIES AND OWNER'S EQUITY	
Short-term Assets:		*Owner's Equity:*	
Cash	$50,000	Owner's Investment	$50,000
Total Assets	$50,000	Total Liabilities and Owner's Equity	$50,000

On the Balance Sheet, only the cash and owner's investment are increased by $50,000. Also note that the Balance Sheet continues to balance—that is, Assets = Liabilities + Owner's Equity.

PURCHASE OF LAND, BUILDING, AND A TRUCK

Next, on January 1, the Bicycle Shoppe buys a piece of land with a building and a truck in order to operate the business. The land has a value of $10,000, the building's value is $25,000, and the truck that will be used for pickups and deliveries is $8,000. All of these values are the actual amounts that the Shoppe pays. Because the Shoppe does not have sufficient cash to pay for all of these assets at the current time, it decides to borrow some money. It pays $23,000 in cash and takes out a mortgage on the land and building for $20,000 to purchase these assets. This is a 20-year loan. Of this loan, $1,000 is due and payable within one year. After these transactions, the Shoppe's Balance Sheet looks like this:

CHRISTINE'S BICYCLE SHOPPE
BALANCE SHEET
JANUARY 1, 1998

ASSETS		LIABILITIES AND OWNER'S EQUITY	
Short-term Assets:		*Short-term Liabilities:*	
Cash	$27,000	Current Portion of Mortgage	$1,000
Total Short-term Assets	$27,000	Total Short-term Liabilities	$1,000
Long-term Assets:		*Long-term Liabilities:*	
Land	$10,000	Mortgage	$19,000
Building	25,000		
Truck	8,000		
Total Long-term Assets	$43,000	Total Liabilities	$20,000
		Owner's Equity:	
		Owner's Investment	$50,000
Total Assets	$70,000	Total Liabilities and Owner's Equity	$70,000

The cash balance has decreased by $23,000, the other assets have increased to $43,000, and the new category in the liabilities column has appeared. The loan of $20,000 has been divided up between the short-term portion of $1,000 and the long-term portion (due in a period of greater than one year) of $19,000. Also, notice that the owner's equity is not affected. As you will see, the owner's equity is affected only when one or more of the following takes place:

- The owner invests more money in the business.
- The business makes a profit or loss.
- The owner takes assets out of the business.

PURCHASE OF INSURANCE

On January 3, the Bicycle Shoppe purchased some insurance on the building. The cost of this insurance is $1,500. Because this purchase covers three years, at this point in the time, the expenditure represents an asset. No time has passed and therefore none of the insurance has been "used up." The Shoppe pays for this insurance with cash. After this transaction, the Shoppe's Balance Sheet looks like this:

CHRISTINE'S BICYCLE SHOPPE
BALANCE SHEET
JANUARY 3, 1998

ASSETS		LIABILITIES AND OWNER'S EQUITY	
Short-term Assets:		*Short-term Liabilities:*	
Cash	$25,500	Current Portion of Mortgage	$1,000
Prepaid Insurance	1,500	*Long-term Liabilities:* Mortgage	$19,000
Total Short-term Assets	$27,000	Total Liabilities	$20,000
Long-term Assets:			
Land	$10,000	*Owner's Equity:*	
Building	25,000	Owner's Investment	$50,000
Truck	8,000		
Total Long-term Assets	$43,000		
Total Assets	$70,000	Total Liabilities and Owner's Equity	$70,000

The only change in the Balance Sheet after the purchase of the insurance is that one asset (cash) has been exchanged for another asset (prepaid insurance) for the exact amount of $1,500.

Orders Bicycles

On January 5, the Bicycle Shoppe orders two different brands of bicycles from two different companies. The Shoppe orders 80 of one kind that cost $100 apiece, and 25 of the other kind that cost $200 apiece. The total cost of the 105 bicycles to the Shoppe is $13,000. This purchase represents an asset known as *inventory*, and it is listed as a short-term asset.

Inventory   An asset held by a business for the purpose of resale.

Inventory is a short-term asset because the Shoppe anticipates selling these 105 bicycles in one year or less. As above, with the purchase of the long-term assets, the Shoppe does not want to pay for all of these bicycles with cash. It pays $10,000 in cash and borrows $3,000 from the seller. This $3,000 becomes an accounts payable of the business, and is shown in the short-term liability section.

Accounts Payable   A short-term liability (debt) incurred from the purchase of inventory or other short-term assets.

After this transaction, the Shoppe's Balance Sheet looks like this:

CHRISTINE'S BICYCLE SHOPPE
BALANCE SHEET
JANUARY 5, 1998

ASSETS		LIABILITIES AND OWNER'S EQUITY	
Short-term Assets:		*Liabilities:*	
Cash	$15,500	Accounts Payable	$3,000
Prepaid Insurance	1,500	Current Portion of Mortgage	1,000
Inventory	13,000	Total Short-term Liabilities	$4,000
		Mortgage Payable	19,000
Total Short-term Assets	$30,000	Total Liabilities	$23,000
Long-term Assets:			
Land	$10,000	*Owner's Equity:*	
Building	25,000	Owner's Investment	$50,000
Truck	8,000		
Total Long-term Assets	$43,000		
Total Assets	$73,000	Total Liabilities and Owner's Equity	$73,000

Once again, the Balance Sheet stays in balance: Assets = Liabilities + Owner's Equity; in other words, $73,000 = $23,000 + $50,000.

The final Balance Sheet does not look identical to the one in Lesson 3 because this Balance Sheet is current as of January 5, 1998, and the one in Lesson 3 is current as of December 31, 1998. This is further evidence that you can prepare a Balance Sheet at any point in time, showing the company's assets, liabilities, and owner's equity.

In this lesson you have seen how various transactions affect the Balance Sheet of a small business. In Lesson 5 you learn some important accounting concepts and the meaning of the Generally Accepted Accounting Principles.

GENERALLY ACCEPTED ACCOUNTING PRINCIPLES

In this lesson you learn the generally accepted rules that guide the practice of preparing financial statements in the United States.

IMPORTANT ACCOUNTING CONCEPTS

Several important concepts have been introduced in the example of Christine's Bicycle Shoppe in the preceding lessons that must be understood before you can say you completely understand the Balance Sheet. You now know the differences between assets, liabilities, and owner's equity. However, it is important that you understand the concepts of *Generally Accepted Accounting Principles* (GAAP), which are the basis for the presentation of these items on the Balance Sheet and are part of the language of accounting and business.

Generally Accepted Accounting Principles (GAAP)   The rules used by accountants to prepare financial statements.

Financial statements must present useful information. If the information is not useful, users of these financial statements will not be able to make proper and correct decisions. In order for the information to be useful, it must be relevant, reliable, understandable, sufficient, and reasonably easy to obtain.

RELEVANT INFORMATION

Relevant information is the information that helps financial statement users to estimate the value of a firm and/or evaluate the firm's management. The statements must be in terms of money since money is our standard means of valuation. In the United States, accountants use the *stable monetary unit* concept. Even though the value of the dollar changes over time (due to inflation), the values that appear on the financial statements are presented at historical cost. This method of accounting ignores the effect of inflation.

Forget About Inflation   Even though arguments could be made for accounting for inflation, the financial statements in the United States are accounted for by using historical cost or "stable monetary units."

Not all information about a firm is relevant for estimating its value or evaluating its management. For example, you don't need to know how many individuals over forty years of age work for the company or what color the machinery is painted in order to make financial decisions about a company.

RELIABLE INFORMATION

To be useful, information must also be reliable. Thus, the information should be verifiable. Sufficient and objective evidence should be available to indicate that the information presented is valid. In addition, the information must not be biased in favor of one statement user or one group of users to the detriment of other statement users. The need for reliable information has caused the federal government to pass laws requiring public companies to have their records and financial statements examined (audited) by independent auditors.

VERIFIABLE INFORMATION

The need for verifiable information does not preclude the use of estimates and approximation. If you were to eliminate from accounting all estimates, the resulting statements would not be useful primarily because the statements would not provide relevant or sufficient information. The estimates or approximations that are used, however, cannot be "wild guesses." They must be based on sufficient evidence that leads the user of the financial statement to believe that the resulting statements provide a reliable basis for evaluating the firm and its management.

UNDERSTANDABLE INFORMATION

To be understandable, the financial information must be comparable. Items on the Balance Sheet that an accountant labels assets or liabilities should be items that statement users would call assets and liabilities. Statement users must compare financial statements of various firms with one another, and they must compare statements of an individual firm with prior years' statements of that same firm in order to make valid decisions. Thus, the accounting practices that a firm uses for a particular transaction should be the same as those used by other firms for the identical transaction. This practice should also be the same practice that the firm used in previous periods. This concept is called *consistency*.

QUANTIFIABLE INFORMATION

Information is easier to understand and use if it is quantified. Thus, accountants use numbers whenever possible, but where it is impossible for some reasons to assign a number to some information, the information (if it is relevant, reliable, understandable, and practicably obtainable) should be presented in narrative form, usually in a footnote to the statements. Narrative information is included because statement users must have sufficient information about a firm. Accountants discuss this idea in terms of the need for adequate or full disclosure.

OBTAINABLE INFORMATION

Furthermore, to be useful, information must be reasonably easy to obtain. Thus, the information must be worth more than it costs to obtain, and must be obtainable on a timely basis. Financial statements must be prepared at least once a year (in many cases, the statements must be prepared quarterly or monthly) and the statements must be issued within a reasonable time after the year ends.

SEPARATE ENTITIES

Financial statements must also present information representing each separate entity. (This idea is called the *Entity Concept*.) In other words, the transactions of each business or person are kept separate from those of other organizations or individuals. Therefore, the transactions of Christine's Bicycle Shoppe are kept separate from the transactions of Christine's personal finances.

> **!** **Strictly Business** Never combine or confuse the transactions of a business with those of its owners.

THE GOING CONCERN

It is always assumed that a company will continue in business for some time into the future. This concept is called the *Going Concern Principle* and is a necessary assumption in order to value the assets. The alternative to the Going Concern Principle is to assume that the business is going bankrupt. When this is known for sure about a business, a different set of accounting principles and rules are used.

REALIZABLE VALUE

Assets should never be shown on the Balance Sheet at more than their realizable value to the company. This concept is called the *Realizable Value Principle*. To do so would probably mislead the statement users into believing that the assets of a firm are worth more than they actually are. For example, if the company has inventory that is listed at a historical cost of $10,000, but due to the economy or the competition or new technology is today only worth $8,000, this asset should be written down and shown on the balance sheet as $8,000.

> **!** **Historical Cost and Realizable Value**   Assets are always shown at historical cost unless the realizable value is less. Accountants in the United States never write assets up if realizable value is higher than historical cost; they only write them down.

MATERIALITY

Financial statements data must be as simple and concise as possible. Any items that are not material should not be included on the statements. If these items were included in the financial statements, they would obscure the important items of interest to the reader. Thus, many immaterial items could be grouped together and called miscellaneous, or the items could be added to (or subtracted from) other items. This concept is called the *Materiality Principle*.

> ! **Materiality Principle** An item is considered material and should be included in the financial statements when its inclusion or exclusion would change the decision of a statement user.

CONSERVATISM

Another accounting principle that accountants use to guide their selection of practices is called *conservatism*. Whenever two or more accounting practices appear to be equally suitable to the transaction under consideration, the accountant should choose the one that results in the lower or lowest asset figure on the Balance Sheet and higher or highest expense on the Income Statement. This practice minimizes net income and owner's equity so as not to be overly optimistic about financial events. The conservatism idea is misused, however, when the accountant chooses a practice that is not as suitable to the situation as an alternative practice merely to report lower assets and higher expenses.

THE SEC, AICPA, FASB, AND GAAP

Congress created the *Securities and Exchange Commission* (SEC) in 1934. At that time, the Commission was given the legal power to prescribe the accounting principles and practices that must be followed by the companies that come within its jurisdiction. Generally speaking, companies come under SEC regulations when they sell securities to the public, list their securities on any one of the securities exchanges (the New

York Stock Exchange or American Exchange, for example), or when they become greater than a specified size as measured by the firm's assets and number of shareholders. Thus, since 1934, the SEC has had the *power* to prepare an "official rule book" of accounting principles or practices that must be followed by almost all companies of any significant size. Yet the Commission has prepared no such book.

Instead, the SEC originally assigned most of the responsibility of identifying or specifying GAAP to the *American Institute of Certified Public Accountants* (AICPA). That role has now been transferred to the *Financial Accounting Standards Board* (FASB). All rulings from the FASB are considered to be GAAP.

A firm must adopt the accounting practices recommended by the FASB or the SEC unless it can identify an alternative practice that has "substantial authoritative support." Even when a company can find "substantial authoritative support" for a practice that differs from the one recommended, the company must include in the financial statement footnotes (or in the auditor's report) a statement indicating that the practices used are not the ones recommended by GAAP. Where practicable, the company must explain how its financial statements would have been different if the company had used Generally Accepted Accounting Principles.

In this lesson you learned the principles that guide the preparation of financial statements. In Lesson 6 you learn how to prepare and use the Income Statement.

THE INCOME STATEMENT

In this lesson you learn how to prepare and use the Income Statement, another of the four required financial statements in use today.

The *Income Statement* presents a summary of revenues and expenses of an entity for a specific period of time, such as a month, a quarter, or a year. This period of time is known as the *accounting period*. The preparation of the Income Statement is different than that of the Balance Sheet because the Balance Sheet represents a single point in time, not a period of time. The Income Statement is also called a *statement of earnings* or a *statement of operations*.

Income Statement A listing of all revenues and expenses of a business during a period of time, usually monthly, quarterly, or yearly.

The preparation of the Income Statement serves several purposes. Oftentimes, the only reason one uses the Income Statement is to concentrate on the "bottom line" or net income (revenue minus expenses). However, Income Statements can also be useful for analyzing changes in the revenue data over a period of time or determining ratios of particular expenses to revenue and how these ratios have changed over certain periods of time.

Don't Be One-Dimensional   Don't concentrate only on one number in the financial statement—net income. The statement contains several other important numbers and ratios.

THE INCOME STATEMENT ILLUSTRATED

Following is an example of an Income Statement for Christine's Bicycle Shoppe at the end of 1998.

CHRISTINE'S BICYCLE SHOPPE
INCOME STATEMENT
FOR THE PERIOD ENDED DECEMBER 31, 1998

Sales	$35,500
Cost of Goods Sold	14,200
Gross Profit	$21,300
Operating Expenses:	
Salaries and Wages	5,200
Bicycle Parts	1,625
Insurance Expense	500
Bad Debt Expense	175

continues

Tools Expense	50
Bank Service Fee	15
Total Operating Expenses	$7,565
Net Income from Operations	$13,735
Other Revenue and Expenses:	
Repair Revenue	3,850
Interest Expense	(2,000)
Net Income Before Taxes	$15,585
Income Taxes	(5,200)
Net Income	$10,385

REVENUE

Revenue (or sales) is the total amount of money obtained by a business from the sale of merchandise or from the rendering of services to its customers. Revenue can come from several sources and thus would generate different words for the general term revenue. That is, a firm can generate revenue from sales, interest, dividends, royalties, or any combination of these. The total revenues of a business are the sum of all of these sources.

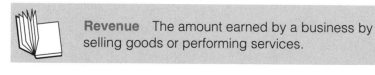

Revenue   The amount earned by a business by selling goods or performing services.

In the example earlier, revenue of $35,500 is from the sales of bicycles.

At this point there has been no discussion of net income. Revenue by itself does not generate net income; it is only one component of net income. Expenses and other items need to be added to or subtracted from revenue to arrive at net income.

> **!** **One Piece in the Puzzle**   Revenue is not equal to net income, but is only one component of net income.

Just as important to note is that revenue is not equal to cash flow. Revenue can be generated prior to a business receiving cash. In other words, a sale can be made and only a promise to pay is generated. Even though the cash will not be collected until some point in the future, the revenue is recognized at the time when the merchandise has been transferred to the buyer, or the services have been performed by the seller. This is often a confusing concept to someone studying accounting for the first time because it presents a new GAAP concept called *recognition.*

> **!** **When to Call It "Revenue"**   Revenue is recognized at the point of the transfer of the merchandise or service, not at the point of receiving the cash.

Thus in our example earlier, the $35,500 in sales was generated by collecting some cash and some promises to pay cash. You cannot tell simply by reading this one number called Sales how much was generated from each of these two sources. But you can tell that at the end of the year, there is still $9,000 owing from the sales (Accounts Receivable at December 31, 1998, on the Balance Sheet) (see Lesson 2). The reason that you cannot tell in total how much was sold on account during the year is that some of the account receivables could have been paid off during the year. Thus the $9,000 only reflects how much is still owed to the business on December 31, 1998.

THE ACCRUAL CONCEPT

This idea of when to recognize revenue on the Income Statement leads to a larger and more pervasive Generally Accepted Accounting Principle, the *Accrual Concept*. The process of recognizing revenue when it is earned and expenses as they are incurred regardless of when the cash changes hands is referred to as the *accrual basis of accounting*. This type of accounting is used by businesses throughout the United Sates for the presentation of their financial statements. However, numerous small firms and most individuals still use the cash basis of accounting to determine their income and income taxes. Under the cash basis of accounting, revenue is not reported until cash is received, and expenses are not reported until cash is disbursed.

The Accrual Basis of Accounting Accounting system that recognizes transactions when revenue, expenses, and purchases take place—whether or not cash changes hands.

OPERATING EXPENSES

Expenses are used to produce the revenues of a business. Expenses represent the cost of doing business.

 Expenses Expenditures that are made to generate revenue.

Examples of expenses are rent, utilities, and salaries. In our current example, the expenses of Christine's Bicycle Shoppe fall under the title of Operating Expenses. These are all of the expenses of the year 1998 that were incurred by the shop in order to generate revenue in the operation of the business. The total is $7,565. Another expense that does not appear in the listing of operating expenses—but that is necessary to generate revenue—is Cost of Goods Sold for $14,200. This expense is listed separately from the others because it is the cost of either the bicycles or the components used to build the bicycles that were sold during 1998.

These bicycles were subsequently sold during the year for $35,500.

An expense is different from an expenditure. An *expenditure* is the spending of cash. All expenses are expenditures; however, all expenditures are not expenses. If the expenditure does not create revenue, it is not an expense. Consider the purchase of a building. When the purchase of a building is made it does not immediately produce revenue. However, over time this building will be used in the production of revenue. When this occurs, the building (and other such assets) depreciate or are used up. The depreciation of the building thus becomes an expense and is matched with those revenues it helped to generate.

> **Does It Generate Revenue?** All expenses are expenditures; however, all expenditures are not expenses. Expenditures are the spending of money. Expenses are only those expenditures that immediately generate revenue.

NET INCOME

Net income represents the difference between those revenues generated during the period and the related expenses that generated that revenue.

> **Net Income** The difference between revenue and expenses for a designated period of time.

Once again note that the term "cash" is not used. Net income does not necessarily generate cash. As with revenue, part of the "bottom line" or net income could be made up of cash, but other parts could be made up of promises to receive cash or promises to pay cash in the future.

> **Income Has Many Faces** Net income is not equal to cash. Financial statements are normally accounted for on the accrual basis; therefore, promises to receive cash and to pay cash are included in the net income figure.

In the earlier example, the words "net income" appear twice. The first time is "Net Income from Operations." This number, $13,735, represents the income earned from selling bicycles, the main product of Christine's Bicycle Shoppe. However, in addition to selling bicycles, Christine also did some repairs. These repairs generated revenue of $3,850 during the year. This revenue appears separately because it is not the main business of this shop.

INTEREST AND INCOME TAXES

Other items subtracted from revenues and expenses before determining the total net income are interest and income taxes. Most accountants classify interest as an "other expense" of the period, not as an operating expense. The reason for this is that interest does not produce revenue, but is only a cost of borrowing money.

In our example, income taxes are $5,200. Most accountants do not consider income taxes to be an expense of the business in that they do not generate revenue for the business. Therefore, the income taxes are usually shown simply as a deduction from total income (revenue minus expenses) before arriving at the net income figure.

After adding the other revenue (from repairs), and subtracting both the interest expense and the income taxes, you see the second use of the term "Net Income." This number, $10,385, represents the total income earned by Christine's Bicycle Shoppe during 1998. This figure is what is often referred to as the "bottom line."

BAD DEBT EXPENSE

The other expense shown in the example is "Bad Debt Expense" of $175. This expense is discussed in Lesson 13.

In this lesson you learned the components of an Income Statement and how they interrelate. You also learned that revenue and net income are not the same as cash because accountants usually use the accrual basis of accounting and not the cash basis. In Lesson 7 you learn how individual transactions affect and change the Income Statement.

TRANSACTIONS THAT AFFECT THE INCOME STATEMENT

In this lesson you learn how individual transactions affect and change the Income Statement.

Lesson 6, "The Income Statement," presented an Income Statement of Christine's Bicycle Shoppe for the period ending December 31, 1998. Referring to this Income Statement, let's examine the transactions that created it.

SALES

During the entire year of 1998, the Bicycle Shoppe sold bicycles for a total sales price of $35,500. Some of these bicycles were sold for cash and some of them were sold for a promise to pay cash in the future. This promise is called *accounts receivable*. The accounts receivable are listed on the Balance Sheet as a short-term asset. By looking at only the Balance Sheet and the Income Statement you are not able to tell how many bicycles were sold for cash and how many were sold for a promise to pay cash in the future. All you can tell at the end of the year is that $8,000 of the accounts receivables are still due and payable to the Bicycle Shoppe.

Now let's look at an individual sale during the year, and see what effect it has on the Income Statement. Let's assume that on January 6, Christine sells two bicycles that had cost her $100 each. She sells the two bicycles for a total of $500. After this transaction the Income Statement would look like this:

CHRISTINE'S BICYCLE SHOPPE
INCOME STATEMENT
FOR THE PERIOD ENDED JANUARY 6, 1998

Sales	$500
Cost of Goods Sold	200
Gross Profit	$300
Expenses	---
Net Income	$300

This transaction has caused two changes to the Income Statement. First, it has increased the revenue account called "Sales" by $500, and second, it has increased an expense account called *Cost of Goods Sold* by the cost of these two bicycles, $200.

At the same time that this transaction has caused a change on the Income Statement, it has also caused the Balance Sheet to change in several ways. Assuming that these bicycles were sold for cash, the asset account (cash) on the Balance Sheet would increase by $500. The asset account inventory, where these bicycles were listed when Christine bought them, would be decreased by the cost of the two bicycles, $200. Remember from Lesson 2, "The Balance Sheet," the items on the Balance Sheet are all listed at their historical cost. In this case, the two bicycles cost Christine's Bicycle Shoppe $200.

The other change on the Balance Sheet (the one that makes this transaction balance) is that retained earnings increases by the difference between the sale price of these two bicycles and the cost. Thus, retained earnings increases by $300 ($500 – $200).

 Net Income   Revenue minus expenses. Net income increases retained earnings on the Balance Sheet.

Now if you were to look at the accounting equation, A = L + OE, it would still balance after this transaction. One asset, cash, has increased by the sale price of $500. Another asset, inventory, has decreased by the cost of the bicycles that were sold, $200. Retained earnings, part of owner's equity, has increased by the difference between the sale price and the cost, or $300. Thus, the left side of this equation has increased by $300 (one asset up $500 and the other down by $200) and the right side of the equation, owner's equity, has increased by the same amount, the net income of $300.

This whole concept is further demonstrated in Lesson 12, "Recording Transactions in the Double Entry Accounting System."

COST OF GOODS SOLD AND GROSS PROFIT

During the complete year of 1998, the cost of all the bicycles sold was equal to $14,200. The difference between the sales price of the bicycles ($35,500) and the cost of these bicycles ($14,200) is called the *gross profit*. In the case of the Bicycle Shoppe, that is equal to $21,300.

OPERATING EXPENSES—PAYING EMPLOYEES

Operating expenses are the costs that are necessary to operate the business on a day-to-day basis. On January 7, Christine's Bicycle Shoppe pays Christine her first week's pay of $100.

> **!** **Don't Mix Business with Pleasure**   Remember that Christine and Christine's Bicycle Shoppe are two separate entities. When the business pays Christine her salary, that is one entity paying the other.

After this transaction, the Income Statement would look like this:

CHRISTINE'S BICYCLE SHOPPE
INCOME STATEMENT
FOR THE PERIOD ENDED JANUARY 7, 1998

Sales	$500
Cost of Goods Sold	200
Gross Profit	$300
Expenses	100
Net Income	$200

The $100 paid to Christine is an expense and as such it is shown in the Income Statement. The net income is decreased by the entire $100, as is the retained earnings and the cash in the Balance Sheet.

SELLING BICYCLES BUT RECEIVING ONLY PARTIAL PAYMENT

On January 21, the Bicycle Shoppe sold 10 more bicycles for a total of $5,000. The cost of these 10 bicycles to the Shoppe was $2,000. The buyers of these bicycles paid a total of $3,500 in cash and promised to pay the other $1,500 within 60 days.

Accounts Receivable An agreement to collect partial or full payment at a later date. In this case, the $1,500 to be paid within 60 days is an accounts receivable.

After this transaction, the Income Statement would look like this:

CHRISTINE'S BICYCLE SHOPPE
INCOME STATEMENT
FOR THE PERIOD ENDED JANUARY 21, 1998

Sales	$5,500
Cost of Goods Sold	2,200
Gross Profit	$3,300
Expenses	100
Net Income	$3,200

On the Income Statement, notice that the entire $5,000 was added to the sales even though only $3,500 cash was received. This step is taken because a transaction has occurred in which the buyers have obligated themselves to pay the full $5,000.

> **!** **Income on Paper**   The income has been earned
> even though the cash has not been received.

The cost of the goods sold increased $2,000 because the 10 bicycles that were sold had cost the business this amount of money (10 bicycles at $200 each).

On the Balance Sheet, the retained earnings increased $3,000. Now you can see that because of the relationship between net income on the Income Statement and retained earnings on the Balance Sheet, any time net income is changed, retained earnings is also changed by the same amount. So that the accounting equation of A = L + OE remains in balance, the asset cash is increased by $3,500, the asset inventory is reduced by the cost of the bicycles or $2,000, and the asset accounts receivable is increased by $1,500. Thus, the net effect on the assets (the left side of the equation) is an increase of $3,000. This change equals the increase in the retained earnings of $3,000 on the right side of the equation.

REPAIRING BICYCLES AND RECEIVING CASH

On February 14, five customers pick up bicycles they had brought into the shop for repair. The customers paid $375 for the repair of these five bicycles. The cost of the parts to repair these bicycles was $105. The customers paid the total amount in cash.

After this transaction, the Income Statement would look like this:

CHRISTINE'S BICYCLE SHOPPE
INCOME STATEMENT
FOR THE PERIOD ENDED FEBRUARY 14, 1998

Sales	$5,500
Cost of Goods Sold	2,200
Gross Profit	$3,300
Expenses	205
Net Income from Operations	$3,095
Other Revenue:	
Repair Revenue	375
Net Income	$3,470

The net income from this transaction of repairing the bicycles is increased by $270, as is the cash and the retained earnings. Also, the total assets owned by the company increased by $270. At this point you should assume that the bicycle parts were bought for cash immediately prior to being used to repair the bicycles. Therefore, there is no inventory of bicycle parts.

OTHER OPERATING EXPENSES

During the year, Christine's Bicycle Shoppe incurred other expenses that were necessary to operate the business. The business had to pay interest on the mortgage that it held. Since the mortgage is for $20,000, and the interest rate on this loan is 10 percent, the total interest paid during the year is $2,000. In addition to the interest, the company bought some small tools to use on the repairs, which cost a total of $1,625, and had to pay a service fee to the bank of $15. The total of these operating expenses increased the expenses on the Income Statement and reduced cash on the Balance Sheet.

At the end of the year, Christine concluded that she was not
going to be able to collect $175 from one of the customers that
had promised to pay. In order to recognize this on the financial statements, she created an expense category called Bad
Debts Expense. This expense is increased by the amount of the
receivable that will not be collected, and the accounts receivable account is reduced by the same amount.

Direct Write-Off Method   The method of writing
off the bad debt directly to the accounts receivable when they are known not to be collected. This
method is used by some businesses today.

Allowance Method   The method of writing off the
bad debt to an allowance account prior to knowing
about an identifiable bad debt. In this method, a
"guesstimate" is made of how much of the total
accounts receivables will not be collected based
on past experience.

Bad Debt Is an Expense   Bad debt expense
reduces the net income in the same way as other
expenses that use cash. Even though this one
does not use cash, it does reduce another asset—
accounts receivable.

The last expense listed on the Income Statement, Insurance
Expense, is another expense that reduces net income without
using cash at the time the expense is recognized. Remember
that in Lesson 4, "Transactions that Affect the Balance Sheet,"
Prepaid Insurance is listed on the Balance Sheet as an asset of

$1,500. This came about because the Bicycle Shoppe bought insurance in advance of using it. By the end of the year, since this was a three-year policy, one-third of it had been used by the business and becomes an expense. To recognize the "using up" of this asset (Prepaid Insurance), the Insurance Expense line is increased by $500. The asset itself is no longer worth the full amount paid, since it now only represents the remaining two years. Therefore, the asset is reduced by the same one-third (one year of the three years), or by $500. If you think back to the accounting equation—A = L + OE—the left-hand side of the equation is reduced by $500 (Prepaid Insurance), and the right side—net income or owner's equity—is also reduced by the same amount, $500.

See Lesson 6 for the listing of all expenses at December 31, 1998 on the Income Statement.

In this lesson you learned how individual transactions affect and change the Income Statement. In Lesson 8 you learn how to prepare and use a Statement of Cash Flows.

8

PREPARING AND USING A STATEMENT OF CASH FLOWS

In this lesson you learn how to prepare and use the Statement of Cash Flows.

WHAT IS A STATEMENT OF CASH FLOWS?

The *Statement of Cash Flows* is one of the four required financial statements. This statement shows where the cash came from and how it was spent during the period of reporting (which may be a month, a quarter, or a year). It also shows the cash flows of the company divided into categories according to three major activities: operating, investing, and financing.

The Statement of Cash Flows differs from the two other financial statements you have learned about so far. The Balance Sheet shows the financial status of a company at the end of the reporting period. Both the Income Statement and the Statement of Cash Flows show the flow of activity during the reporting period. The Income Statement reports this activity on the accrual basis and the Statement of Cash Flows reports it on the cash basis.

The Purpose of the Statement

Like the other required financial statements you have learned about—the Balance Sheet and the Income Statement—the Statement of Cash Flows enables users to make decisions about the company. In reviewing a Statement of Cash Flows, you can predict the ability of the company to pay dividends and interest in the future and view the relationship between cash and net income.

> **!** **Income Doesn't Always Mean Cash** Remember that a company can earn a large amount of income and have little or no cash at the end of an accounting period.

Cash and Cash Equivalents

In business, the term "cash" has a broader meaning than the amount of cash in the bank at the end of the year. It is also defined as the liquid short-term investments that can quickly be converted into cash within a very short period of time. Examples of *cash equivalents* are certificates of deposit, money market accounts, and U.S. Government Treasury Bills. Therefore, whenever the term "cash" is used in this lesson, it refers to cash and all cash equivalents.

THE STATEMENT OF CASH FLOWS ILLUSTRATED

By looking at the Balance Sheet, you can see how much cash Christine's Bicycle Shoppe has at the end of 1998—$17,385.

CHRISTINE'S BICYCLE SHOPPE
STATEMENT OF CASH FLOWS
FOR THE PERIOD ENDED DECEMBER 31, 1998

Cash Flow from Operating Activities:	
Net Income	$10,385
Increase in Accounts Receivable	(9,000)
Increase in Inventory	(13,000)
Increase in Prepaid Insurance	(1,000)
Increase in Accounts Payable	3,000
Total Cash Flow from Operations	($9,615)
Cash Flow from Investing Activities:	
Purchase of Land	($10,000)
Purchase of Building	(25,000)
Purchase of Truck	(8,000)
Total Cash Flow from Investing Activities	($43,000)
Cash Flow from Financing Activities:	
Borrowing for the Mortgage	$20,000
Owner's Investment	50,000
Total Cash Flow from Financing Activities	$70,000
Net increase in Cash and Cash Equivalents	$17,385

Note: Parentheses indicate decreases in cash.

OPERATING ACTIVITIES

The first section of the cash flow statement shows how much cash was generated from the day-to-day operations of the business—that is, from operations. This statement always begins with net income and then adds and subtracts items from operations that cause cash to increase or decrease.

In this example, accounts receivable has increased from a beginning balance of $0 to an ending balance of $9,000. Remember, net income = revenue – expenses. Since not all of these sales (revenue) were cash customers, you must subtract the sales on credit (accounts receivable) from net income to determine the amount of cash generated from these sales.

> **!** **The Cash Amount Varies**   Net income may or may not have increased the cash account.

Inventory also has increased from a beginning balance of $0 to $13,000 at the end of the year. This change indicates an increase in one asset, inventory, and a decrease in another, cash (in order to buy that inventory). Because the inventory purchase used cash (later you will adjust for the portion that was purchased on account), you must subtract the increase in inventory in order to determine the cash generated from operations. The reduction to net income in our example is $13,000.

Prepaid insurance represents the purchase with cash of insurance that is going to be used in the future. In this example,

Christine's Bicycle Shoppe has paid $1,500 in cash for this asset. Since this policy was for three years, at the end of 1998, one-third of this asset was used up. The remaining asset of prepaid insurance covers an additional two years. The $500 that represents the insurance coverage for 1998 is shown on the Income Statement as an operating expense, and correspondingly has reduced the asset prepaid insurance. The remaining balance in the prepaid insurance account of $1,000 represents an outflow of cash that is not included on the Income Statement. For this reason it needs to be subtracted from Net Income in the Operating Activities section.

The balance in the accounts payable account has increased from the beginning of the year when it was $0 to an ending balance of $3,000. This account represents the purchase of inventory (bicycles) on account. Purchases are part of the expense account called Cost of Goods Sold. The portion of purchases that were on account and did not use cash this period needs to be added back to net income to determine the cash generated from operations. In our example, this is the reason for the $3,000 adjustment.

When all of these adjustments are made to net income, the total represents the cash flow from operations in this example to be a negative cash flow of $9,615.

INVESTING ACTIVITIES

Any time a company makes a purchase of property, plant, or equipment, this addition is treated as an investment in the organization. This investment represents a cash flow from the company. Even though the entire purchase may not have been with cash, but with some borrowed money, the entire purchase is shown as a cash flow in the investing section of the cash flow statement, and any borrowing of money is shown separately in the financing section.

In the example earlier, Christine's Bicycle Shoppe purchased three long-term assets during the year 1998. The land for $10,000, the building for $25,000, and the truck for $8,000 are all shown as negative cash flows in the investing activities section of the cash flows statement.

The total of these three purchases represents the total cash flow from investing activities of $43,000.

FINANCING ACTIVITIES

Financing activities represent the cash that has come into or out of the company for the purpose of financing all of the other activities. Accounts such as Mortgage Payable, Common Stock, and Retained Earnings represent the basis of these activities. The cash amounts of these financing activities are calculated by analyzing these accounts.

In the earlier example, Christine invested $50,000 into the business on the first day. This investment was in cash and is thus shown as an increase in the cash flow from financing activities. In addition to this investment by the owner (Christine), a 15-year loan was negotiated in order to purchase the land and the building. This loan for $20,000 is also shown as an inflow of cash to the business and thus an increase in cash flow from financing activities.

The total of these two items, $70,000, represents the total cash flow into the company from financing activities during the year 1998.

The total of the three cash flows—from operations, from investing, and from financing—represents the total increase or decrease in cash and cash equivalents for the business during the year being reported (in this example, an increase of $17,385). Notice that this total represents the change in cash from the beginning of the year to the end of the year. In our example, cash at the beginning of the year was $0, and at the end was $17,385.

In this lesson you learned how to prepare the Statement of Cash Flows. In Lesson 9 you learn how the accounting for corporations differs from that of an individual proprietorship.

THE CORPORATION

In this lesson you learn how the accounting for a corporation differs from that of an individual proprietorship.

Until now you have been working with Christine's Bicycle Shoppe, which is an *individual proprietorship*. In other words, the business has one owner, and she has invested some of her own money into the company as well as borrowing some additional money.

A *corporation* has been defined as "an artificial being" independent from its owners. It is a legal separate entity. Corporations can be set up as for-profit or not-for-profit. For-profit corporations depend on making money in order to continue into the future. Not-for-profit corporations do not depend upon profit to continue. Examples of not-for-profit corporations include charities and governmental, educational, and recreational organizations. These types of business, rather than depending on profit, depend on gifts and grants from the public and private sectors for their continuation.

A corporation is given the right to operate (a charter) from the state in which it wants to incorporate. However, just because it is incorporated in one state, does not mean that it cannot operate in the others. Due to differing tax laws, and the

incorporation fees, some states have become more advanta-
geous to incorporate in than others.

CHARACTERISTICS OF A CORPORATION

Several characteristics differentiate a corporation from other
forms of business. One of the characteristics of a corporation
that distinguishes it from a partnership or a proprietorship
is that the creditors of a corporation can lay claim only to
the assets of the corporation. Creditors of partnerships or
proprietorships, on the other hand, can turn to the personal
assets of each owner whenever the assets of the unincorpo-
rated firm are not sufficient to meet the creditors' claims. Because of this corporate characteristic, the states have laws that
restrict the stockholders' right to withdraw assets from the
corporation. Each state has a law that prevents a corporation
from paying dividends (that is, owners withdrawing assets)
whenever the net assets (assets minus liabilities) are at or below a certain level. This minimum net asset figure is often
called the *legal capital* of a corporation.

CAPITAL STOCK

When a corporation receives its charter from the state, it also
receives the right to sell a particular number of shares of stock
to the public. This number of shares is called the *authorized
shares*. The corporation can sell as many shares as it chooses
up to this authorized amount, but no more.

Usually, two types of *capital stock* can be authorized by the
state—common stock and preferred stock. The common and
preferred stock may or may not have a par value. If a stock
has a *par value*, that value appears on the stock certificate (for

example, $1.00 par or $5.00 par or $100.00 par, and so on) and in many states the total par value of all stock sold is the corporation's legal capital. In some states, however, a corporation's legal capital is equal to the total amount received when the stock is initially sold. Par-value stock often is sold for more than the par-value figure.

Generally speaking, common stock differs from preferred stock in four ways:

- Common stockholders have the right to vote for the directors of the corporation; preferred shareholders usually do not.

- Preferred shareholders have first claim to dividends; that is, in any year that dividends are declared by the board of directors, preferred shareholders must be allocated their share of the dividends before the common stockholders are entitled to any.

- The preferred shareholders have a fixed claim to dividends during any one year, whereas the common shareholders' claims are not fixed.

- In the event the corporation is liquidated (that is, its assets are sold, liabilities paid off, and the remaining cash distributed to the shareholders), the preferred shareholders' claim to the corporate assets takes precedence over those of the common shareholders.

Preferred stock has two other interesting characteristics. Most preferred stock is *cumulative*. This means that if the preferred shareholders are not paid their full dividend in any year, in subsequent years dividend payments to the preferred shareholders must be sufficient to cover the previously inadequate dividend payments before any dividends can be paid to the common stockholders.

> ❗ **A Cumulative Example** A 10 percent preferred stock with a par value of $100 should receive a $10 dividend each year. If only $6 is paid in year one, the remaining $4 plus the $10 for the following year must be paid before the common stockholders receive any dividend.

When dividends on cumulative preferred stock are not paid, those dividends are said to be in arrears, and a footnote must be added to the financial statements indicating the amount of the dividends in arrears. The Balance Sheet does not show dividends in arrears as a liability. Some preferred stock is noncumulative, which means that if a year passes and the preferred stockholders do not receive a dividend, those shareholders never receive that dividend payment.

Some preferred stock is *participating preferred,* which means that the preferred shareholders' claim to dividends in any one year is not rigidly fixed. Those shareholders, in certain "good" years, share with the common shareholders in the "excess" dividend payments. The amount or percentage of dividends that the preferred shareholders can receive in excess of the amount to which they have a prior claim varies considerably from company to company.

> ❗ **Sharing the Wealth** A 10 percent, $100 par value preferred stock receives a $10 dividend. The common stock receives in the same year a 10 percent dividend. The preferred stockholders and the common stockholders will then receive 50 percent of the remainder of the dividend pool declared by the board of directors.

This agreement represents only one example of one type of participation. The level of participation can be anything written by the board of directors, including no participation at all.

! **Where Does the Money from the Sale of Stock Go?**   When stock is initially sold to the public, the corporation receives the money. After the initial sale, when the stock is sold by one individual to another (on a stock market such as the New York Stock Exchange or the Over The Counter Exchange), the money does not affect the assets of the corporation.

THE STOCKHOLDERS' EQUITY SECTION OF THE BALANCE SHEET

As you might recall, the Stockholders' Equity section of the Balance Sheet contains two items, Owner's Investment and Retained Earnings. The only difference on the books of a corporation is that the Owner's Investment is replaced with Common Stock and Preferred Stock. The reason for this is that the owners of the corporation are the stockholders and not an individual.

DIVIDENDS AND SPLITS

Owners of a corporation, the shareholders, can legally receive a distribution of the assets of the corporation in two ways.

First, the corporation can be liquidated—that is, all the liabilities are paid off and the remaining assets distributed to the shareholders, which means that the corporation ceases to operate. Second, the corporation can pay dividends. In general, a corporation cannot pay a dividend when such action would reduce the corporation's capital below its legal capital figure. Usually, dividends can be paid, but only to the extent of the total retained earnings.

In addition, a corporation obviously cannot pay a cash dividend unless it has the cash, and the cash is not needed for other purposes. Often a corporation has sizable retained earnings as a result of successful operations in the past, but very little cash.

Dividends can be divided into two categories, cash and stock. Only when the board of directors declares dividends do the dividends become legal liabilities of the corporation. Once the dividends are declared, the corporation is legally required to pay these dividends or issue the additional shares within a specified period of time. Companies often declare and issue *stock dividends* instead of cash dividends. When this occurs, the company issues additional shares of stock in the corporation.

A company can also declare a stock split. The *stock split* increases the number of shares outstanding and decreases the stocks' par value. Stock may be split in a variety of ways—for example, 2 for 1, 3 for 1, 3 for 2, and so on. Whether the company issues a stock dividend or a stock split, it must have the additional shares authorized by the state prior to the issue. It is possible this has already occurred; the company may have had 10,000 shares authorized when it was chartered, and has issued only 3,000 shares to date. If not enough stock remains from the initial authorization, the company must request a larger authorization from the state.

A company might split its stock for several reasons. One reason is that a stock split increases the number of shares on the market, which may mean that, in time, more people will own a part of the company. Another is that the more shares outstanding, the less the price per share; so again, more people are able to buy the shares. Yet another reason is that many people would rather buy 100 shares (a round lot) of $50 stock than 50 shares (less than 100 shares is considered to be an odd lot) of $100 stock even though the proportion of the company they would own would be the same. One reason for this decision is that the brokerage fee on round lots (one hundred shares or multiples thereof) is less than on odd lots.

TREASURY STOCK

When a company buys back its own stock and does not cancel it or resell it, it is known as *treasury stock*. A company may buy its own stock for a variety of reasons. It may need the stock to distribute for stock dividends or as part of a stock option contract with its employees.

In this lesson you learned how the financial statements in a corporation differ from those of a proprietorship. In Lesson 10 you learn how individual transactions affect and change financial statements of a corporation.

TRANSACTIONS THAT AFFECT THE CORPORATION

In this lesson you learn how individual transactions affect the financial statements of a corporation.

SALE OF STOCK

When a corporation sells stock, cash is increased (if the stock was sold for cash) and the common stock account is increased by the same amount. For example, when 100 shares of common stock with a par value of $20 is sold for $5,000 cash, cash is increased $5,000, the common stock account increases $2,000, and another account called *Paid-in Capital—Common* (or *Capital in Excess of Par*) is increased by $3,000.

The impact on the Balance Sheet appears as follows:

Current Assets:		*Stockholders' Equity:*	
Cash	$5,000	Common Stock, $20 Par	$2,000
		Paid-in Capital in Excess of Par—Common	3,000
			$5,000

> **Categorizing Value in Excess of Par**   When stock sells for more than its par value, the stock account on the Balance Sheet increases by the par value of the stock. Any excess over the par value is added to another account titled Paid-in Capital in Excess of Par—Common.

When stock does not have a par value, but the Board of Directors has assigned a stated value to the no-par stock, the stock sale transaction is accounted for as shown in the preceding example. The amount added to the stock account equals the total stated value of the stock sold, and any excess is added to the paid-in capital account.

When stock has neither a par value nor a stated value, the stock item is increased by whatever amount is realized upon the sale of the stock. For example, if 10 shares of no-par common stock sell for $100, the common stock account is increased by $100; if 10 more shares are sold for $115 a few days later, the common stock account increases another $115, and so on.

Stock rarely, if ever, is initially sold by a corporation for less than par or stated value, either because state laws prevent such a sale or because the laws allow the creditors of the corporation to hold stockholders personally liable to the extent of any such discount.

The sale of preferred stock would cause the same changes as shown in the example, with the exception that the title of the accounts would be Preferred Stock and Paid-in Capital in Excess of Par—Preferred instead.

PAYMENT OF CASH DIVIDENDS

When the board of directors declares cash dividends, the retained earnings figure is decreased and dividends payable, a current liability, is increased. For example, if a corporation has 150,000 shares of common stock outstanding and the board of directors declares a $.20 dividend, the retained earnings would decrease by $30,000 and the dividends payable increase by $30,000.

BALANCE SHEET CHANGES

Current Liabilities:	
Dividends Payable	+$30,000
Stockholders' Equity:	
Common Stock	no effect
Retained Earnings	-$30,000
No Change	0

The income statement is not affected.

When the dividend is paid, cash is decreased and dividends payable is decreased. In the preceding example, when the dividend is paid, cash would decrease $30,000 and the liability "dividends payable" would be eliminated from the Balance Sheet.

Financial statements are affected in the same manner when cash dividends are declared and paid to preferred shareholders.

STOCK DIVIDENDS

Assume the stockholders' equity section of a corporation looked like this:

Stockholders' Equity:

Common Stock, $50 Par	$5,000,000
Paid-in Capital In Excess of Par—Common	3,500,000
	$8,500,000
Retained Earnings	10,000,000
Total Stockholders' Equity	$18,500,000

The company declared and issued a 10 percent stock dividend when its stock was selling on the market for $200 per share. You can see from the stockholders' equity section that the company had 100,000 shares of common stock outstanding prior to the stock dividend ($5,000,000 common stock / $50 par = 100,000 shares). A 10 percent stock dividend will increase the number of shares by 10,000. Since the market price of each share is $200, the retained earnings account is decreased by $2,000,000 (10,000 shares × $200 = $2,000,000), the common stock account is increased by $500,000 (10,000 shares × $50 Par = $500,000), and the paid-in capital account is increased by the difference, which is $1,500,000.

The equity section of the Balance Sheet appears as follows after the stock dividend:

Stockholders' Equity:

Common Stock, $50 Par	$5,500,000
Paid-in Capital In Excess of Par—Common	5,000,000
	$10,500,000
Retained Earnings	8,000,000
Total Stockholders' Equity	$18,500,000

Notice that the total stockholders' equity does not change ($18,500,000). Furthermore, neither the assets nor the liabilities of the company are affected by a stock dividend nor are the income or expense items.

The accounting for a stock dividend is somewhat different whenever the dividend is greater than 20 to 25 percent of the shares previously outstanding. Had the company in the preceding example declared and issued a stock dividend of 50 percent instead of 10 percent, for example, the Balance Sheet would have been changed to look like this:

Stockholders' Equity:

Common Stock, $50 Par	$7,500,000
Paid-in Capital In Excess of Par—Common	3,500,000
	$11,000,000
Retained Earnings	7,500,000
Total Stockholders' Equity	$18,500,000

Whenever large stock dividends (greater than 20 to 25 percent) are issued, the market value of the stock is not relevant in determining the change in the Balance Sheet figures. Instead, the retained earnings are reduced by the par value of the new shares. In the preceding example, the new shares had a total par value of $2,500,000 (50,000 shares × $50 = $2,500,000).

STOCK SPLITS

Assume that the board of directors of the company above declared a two-for-one stock split instead of a stock dividend. Two hundred thousand shares (remember, there were 100,000 shares outstanding) of new $25 par stock would have been sent to the shareholders and the old $50 par stock would have been called in. Only the Stockholders' Equity section of the Balance Sheet would change, and it would look like this:

Stockholders' Equity:

Common Stock, $25 Par	$5,000,000
Paid-in Capital in Excess of Par—Common	3,500,000
	$8,500,000
Retained Earnings	10,000,000
Total Stockholders' Equity	$18,500,000

Notice that there are no changes except that the par value has changed from $50 to $25.

Treasury Stock

Assume that the "T" Corporation sold 300,000 shares of $10 par stock for $15 each on July 1, 1998, the day it began doing business. Two years later, it bought back 10,000 shares of its own stock for $200,000. Until this stock is legally canceled or resold, it is known as treasury stock.

Before the "T" Corporation acquired its own stock, its Stockholders' Equity section of the Balance Sheet looked like this:

Stockholders' Equity:

Common Stock, $10 Par	$3,000,000
Paid-in Capital in Excess of Par—Common	1,500,000
	$4,500,000
Retained Earnings	600,000
Total Stockholders' Equity	$5,100,000

After the "T" Corporation acquired 10,000 shares of its own stock, its Stockholders' Equity section of the Balance Sheet looked like this:

Stockholders' Equity:

Common Stock, $10 Par	
(10,000 Shares of which are Treasury Stock)	$3,000,000
Paid-in Capital—Common	1,500,000
	$4,500,000
Retained Earnings[1]	600,000
	$5,100,000
Less: Cost of Treasury Stock	(200,000)
Total Stockholders' Equity	$4,900,000

[1]*Although the retained earnings total $600,000, the "T" Corporation may legally declare and pay dividends of not more than $400,000. The acquisition of treasury stock has reduced the retained earnings available for dividends by $200,000, the cost of the treasury stock.*

You should be aware of several changes caused by the purchase of treasury stock:

- The total stockholders' equity has decreased from $5,100,000 to $4,900,000. The Balance Sheet is still in balance because cash has decreased by the same amount.

- A treasury stock purchase reduces the amount of dividends the corporation can pay. The transaction restricts the retained earnings. This restriction is necessary to prevent a corporation from reducing its capital below its required legal capital figure. For the same reason, a corporation usually cannot buy treasury stock unless its retained earnings are equal to or exceed the cost of the treasury stock.

- Footnote [1] becomes an integral part of the Balance Sheet. The Balance Sheet would not be complete without either this footnote or some similar type notation in the Stockholders' Equity section of the statement.

- The treasury stock is not an asset. The purchase of the stock by the corporation merely reduces the amount that the owners have invested in the business.

- The number of shares of common stock now outstanding is 290,000 shares.

If cash dividends were declared today, they would be paid only to the owners of the 290,000 shares; the company would not pay dividends to itself. Dividends are paid only on outstanding stock; treasury stock is not considered to be outstanding (in the preceding example, the "T" Corporation has issued 300,000 shares but only 290,000 shares are outstanding).

In addition to issued and outstanding stock, each corporation is authorized to issue a certain number of shares as specified in the corporate charter. The number of shares authorized can be greater than or equal to the number of shares issued, but a company can issue no more shares than authorized. Most firms show the number of shares authorized, issued, and outstanding in the Stockholder's Equity section of the Balance Sheet. For example, before the purchase of the treasury stock, the "T" Corporation's Stockholders' Equity section may report:

Stockholders' Equity:

Common Stock, $10 Par

Authorized 500,000 Shares

Issued & Outstanding 300,000

Shares	$3,000,000
Paid-in Capital in Excess of Par—Common	1,500,000
	$4,500,000
Retained Earnings	600,000
Total Stockholders' Equity	$5,100,000

After the purchase of the 10,000 shares of treasury stock, the "T" Corporation's Stockholders' Equity section would look like this:

Stockholders' Equity:

Common Stock, $10 Par (10,000 Shares of which are Treasury Stock)

Authorized 500,000 Shares

Issued 300,000 Shares

Outstanding 290,000 Shares	$3,000,000
Paid-in Capital in Excess of Par—Common	1,500,000
	$4,500,000
Retained Earnings[1] 600,000	$5,100,000
Less: Cost of Treasury Stock	(200,000)
Total Stockholders' Equity	$4,900,000

[1]*Although the retained earnings total $600,000, the "T" Corporation may legally declare and pay dividends of not more than $200,000. The acquisition of treasury stock has reduced the retained earnings available for dividends by $200,000, the cost of the treasury stock.*

The company can either sell or cancel its treasury stock. If the "T" Corporation sold 4,000 shares of its treasury stock for $25 per share, its Stockholders' Equity section would look like this:

Stockholders' Equity:

Common Stock, $10 Par (6,000 Shares of which are Treasury Stock)

Authorized 500,000 Shares

Issued 300,000 Shares

Outstanding 294,000 Shares	$3,000,000
Paid-in Capital in Excess of Par—Common	1,500,000
Paid-in Capital in Excess of Par—Treasury	20,000
	$4,520,000
Retained Earnings (See [1] in the preceding stockholders' equity section)	600,000
	$5,120,000
Less: Cost of Treasury Stock	(120,000)
Total Stockholders' Equity	$5,000,000

You should notice the following:

- The total stockholders' equity increased by $100,000—the amount of cash received for the sale of the treasury stock.

- The Treasury Stock item decreased by only $80,000, the amount the 4,000 shares had cost the company when they were purchased: 4,000 shares × $20 per share.

- The sale of treasury stock for more than it cost (here, sales price was $100,000 and the cost was $80,000) did not result in a profit of $20,000.

The Income Statement is not affected by the transaction. The retained earnings do not change; the $20,000 creates a new Balance Sheet account called Paid-in Capital—Treasury. This account is somewhat like the Paid-in Capital—Common account that results when stock is initially sold for more than its par value.

When treasury stock is sold for less than it cost, the Paid-in Capital—Treasury account is reduced. If this account does not exist or if the account is not large enough to absorb the difference between the sales prices and the cost of the treasury stock, the Paid-In Capital in Excess of Par—Common is reduced. If this account is not sufficient, retained earnings are reduced.

In this lesson you learned how individual transactions affect the financial statements of a corporation. In Lesson 11 you find out who the auditors are, what type of reports they issue, and why those reports are useful to you.

AUDITORS AND AUDITS

In this lesson you learn who the different types of auditors are, the purpose of their audits, and the different types of reports that are issued.

TYPE OF AUDITORS

An *auditor* is an individual who checks the accuracy and fairness of the accounting records of a company and determines whether the company is in accordance with a set of rules. The individual who does the audit can work for various types of organizations. The following three sections discuss the three major types of auditors.

THE CERTIFIED PUBLIC ACCOUNTANT (CPA)

Certified Public Accountants are auditors who serve the needs of the general public. The work of these individual CPAs and firms of auditors includes auditing, tax planning and preparation, and management consulting. These firms of CPAs range in size from one individual to international partnerships with more than 2,000 partners.

The largest of these firms have offices worldwide, and are referred to as the "Big Six." Even though they employ only about 12 percent of all CPAs in the United States, the Big Six actually perform the audits of about 85 percent of the largest corporations in the world.

Individuals who act as an independent auditor (CPA) must be licensed to perform audits by the state in which they practice. The laws vary from state to state as to the requirements that must be met in order to obtain such licenses. However, to be issued a license to practice as a CPA, all states require the person to pass a uniform examination that is prepared and graded by the American Institute of CPAs (AICPA). In addition to passing this examination, individuals in most states must have some experience working with another CPA prior to being licensed. Most states also require that after an individual is licensed to practice as a public accountant, she must have a minimum amount of continuing education each year in order to have her license renewed.

INTERNAL AUDITORS

Internal auditors are employed by companies to audit the records of that company. The functions of these auditors vary greatly, depending upon the needs and expectations of management. In general, the work includes compliance audits (making sure the accounting is in compliance with the rules of the company and the laws under which it operates) and operational audits (a review of an organization's operating procedures for efficiency and effectiveness).

As with CPAs, many internal auditors are also certified by passing a nationally prepared examination. This examination is for the Certificate of Internal Auditing and is prepared by the Institute of Internal Auditors.

In order for the internal auditor to be independent, he needs to report to the highest level of responsibility within the company. This may include the Board of Directors or the Audit Committee of the Board of Directors.

Internal Auditors work closely with the external auditors (the CPAs) in order to reduce the amount of time that the outside auditor needs to spend with the company.

GOVERNMENTAL AUDITORS

Governmental auditors, as you would expect, are individuals who perform the audit function as described earlier, but for a governmental organization. As with the other two types of auditors described here, these individuals also must be independent from the individuals or groups they are auditing.

Many different governmental organizations commonly hire and use auditors, including the United States General Accounting Office (GAO). The major function of this group is to perform the audit function for Congress. The Internal Revenue Service hires auditors to enforce the federal tax laws as defined by the Congress and interpreted by the courts. Several other governmental organizations hire auditors to ensure that the regulations affecting those entities under their jurisdictions are met. Some of these include the Bureau of Alcohol, Tobacco, and Firearms (ATF); the Drug Enforcement Agency (DEA); and the Federal Bureau of Investigation (FBI).

DIFFERENCE BETWEEN ACCOUNTING AND AUDITING

Accounting, which you have learned about in all of the previous lessons, is the process of recording, classifying, and summarizing economic events in a process that leads to the preparation of financial statements.

Auditing, on the other hand, is not concerned with the preparation of the accounting data, but with the evaluation of this data to determine if it is properly presented in accordance with the rules of accounting and whether it properly reflects the events that have occurred during the period.

WHAT IS AN AUDIT?

One of the rules that the Securities and Exchange Commission (SEC) has issued is that an independent public accountant must audit the financial statements of public companies (those companies selling stock to the public). This rule means that an accountant, who is not an employee of the company and who is licensed to practice as a public accountant by the state where the financial statements are being prepared, must examine or audit the records of the company. This accountant must also determine whether or not the financial statements are in accordance with the rules of Generally Accepted Accounting Principles (GAAP).

Auditing   The accumulation and evaluation of evidence about a company in order to issue a report about that company.

A typical auditor's report (known as the unqualified report) is issued when the financial statements are in accordance with GAAP. This report is written and issued by the auditors and is submitted to the public with the financial statements.

> **!** **Financial Statements Are Done Internally**   It is important to remember that the financial statements are prepared by the management of the company and not by the auditors.

THE STANDARD AUDIT OPINION ILLUSTRATED

The standard unqualified audit opinion is the most common report issued. It is used in the majority of all reports. It is issued under the following situations:

1. All financial statements are included.

2. These financial statements are prepared in accordance with GAAP.

3. The auditor has gathered sufficient evidence to give an opinion on these statements.

4. The auditor is independent of the company being audited.

5. The auditor has followed the generally accepted rules of auditing called Generally Accepted Auditing Standards (GAAS).

The Generally Accepted Auditing Standards are spelled out in the Standards of the accounting profession. Here is another example of the SEC and the AICPA's complementing each other to help ensure that the financial statements issued to the public present useful information, information that is relevant, reliable, understandable, and sufficient for use in making decisions about the firms and their management.

When these five conditions are met, a report such as the following is issued. Notice that the report is on a comparative basis, and therefore the management of the company must attach two years' worth of financial statements.

SYDNEY AND MAUDE
CERTIFIED PUBLIC ACCOUNTANTS
7 CIRCLE DRIVE
CAPE COD, MA 02117

Independent Auditor's Report
To the Stockholders
The Las Brisas Company

We have audited the accompanying Balance Sheets of The Las Brisas Company as of December 31, 1998 and 1997, and the related statements of income, retained earnings, and cash flows for the years then ended. These financial statements are the responsibility of the Company's management. Our responsibility is to express an opinion on these financial statements based on our audits.

We conducted our audits in accordance with generally accepted auditing standards. Those standards require that we plan and perform the audit to obtain reasonable assurance about whether the financial statements are free of material misstatement. An audit includes examining, on a test basis, evidence supporting the amounts and disclosures in the financial statements. An audit also includes assessing the accounting principles used and significant estimates made by management, as well as evaluating the overall financial statement presentation. We believe that our audits provide a reasonable basis for our opinion.

In our opinion, the financial statements referred to above present fairly, in all material respects, the financial position of the Las Brisas Company as of December 31, 1998 and 1997, and the results of its operations and its cash flows for the years then ended in conformity with Generally Accepted Accounting Principles.

Sydney and Maude, CPAs
March 17, 1999

THE PARTS OF THE REPORT

Every standard audit report is composed of seven parts. They include:

1. The report title ("Independent Auditor's Report")

2. The audit report address ("To the Stockholders")

3. Introductory paragraph ("We have audited...")

4. Scope paragraph ("We conducted our audits...")

5. Opinion paragraph ("In our opinion...")

6. Name of CPA firm ("Sydney and Maude, CPAs")

7. Audit report date ("March 17, 1999"). This date represents when the work on the audit was completed, not the date the report was issued. Depending on the size of the company being audited, the review of the evidence may take two to three months.

The wording of this report may vary slightly from auditor to auditor, but the meaning remains the same.

Other Types of Audit Reports

There are three other types of audit reports you might encounter when reviewing financial statements:

- **Qualified Audit Report:** Issued by the auditor when he or she concludes that the financial statements are presented in accordance with GAAP, except for some specified items being different.

- **Adverse Audit Report:** Issued by the auditor when he or she concludes that the financial statements are not presented fairly and are not in accordance with the rules of accounting (GAAP).

- **Disclaimer Audit Report:** Issued by the auditor when he or she does not have enough information to determine whether the financial statements are in accordance with the accounting rules. The auditor also issues this type of report if he or she is not independent of the company being audited.

Why Audits Are Useful to You

As the business world becomes more global and complex, so do the financial reports being issued by the management of companies. The information provided and the rules that govern their presentation have exploded during the past 20 years. Today it is becoming more and more difficult for the layperson (non-accountant) to fully understand these presentations.

The auditor's report of a company's financial statements gives the reader and user of these financial statements an assurance that this information is in accordance with a set of rules (GAAP) established and reviewed by a source (the auditor) who is objective and independent of company management.

> **!** **Audits Are GAAP-Based**   These audits do not guarantee the accuracy or predictive ability of these financial statements, only that they are presented in accordance with a set of accounting rules (GAAP).

By having an independent audit, the user—you—can be assured that the information is free of material errors and fraud. This assurance thus allows you to make investment and analytical decisions about the company being reviewed.

In this lesson you learned who auditors are, what an audit is, the different types of audit reports that auditors issue, and how these audits can be helpful for you. In Lesson 12 you learn how to use the double entry system of accounting.

RECORDING TRANSACTIONS IN THE DOUBLE ENTRY ACCOUNTING SYSTEM

In this lesson you learn how to record business transactions into the accounting records.

THE GENERAL JOURNAL

Some time after an accountable business transaction has occurred, it is recorded in a book called a *general journal*. A general journal is often referred to as the *book of original entry* because the journal is a book in which a transaction is first recorded. While there are many different kinds of journals, it is most important to focus on the general journal.

The pages of a general journal will look something like this:

GENERAL JOURNAL

DATE	ENTRIES	REFERENCE	AMOUNTS DEBITS	CREDITS

The word "debit" refers to the left side of the amount columns and the word "credit" identifies the right side of the amount columns. Debit does not mean something unfavorable nor does credit mean something favorable, as some non-accountants often believe.

JOURNAL ENTRIES

To illustrate how transactions are recorded in the general journal, you can use the transaction described in Lesson 4. To help understand debits and credits, refer to the accounting equation A = L + OE.

Assets, or the left side of the equation, are increased with debits and decreased with credits. The right side of the equation, the liabilities and the owner's equity items, are just the opposite: They are increased with credits and decreased with debits. By using this system, the accounting equation stays in balance because you are increasing or decreasing both sides of the equation by equal amounts. In addition, if you increase or decrease the debits by the same amount as you increase or decrease the credits on each transaction, you have accomplished the second goal of bookkeeping—making sure that the debits always equal the credits.

 Debits   Debits increase the left side of the equation (A = L + OE) and *credits* decrease the left side. The right side of the equation is just the opposite: Debits decrease the liabilities and owner's equity and credits increase them.

The table below summarizes this concept:

	DEBIT	CREDIT
Assets	↑	↓
Liabilities	↓	↑
Owner's Equity	↓	↑
Revenue	↓	↑
Expenses	↑	↓

Now let's record some of the transactions of the previous lessons. First, Christine invested $50,000 in her bicycle shop. This transaction would be recorded as follows:

GENERAL JOURNAL

			AMOUNTS	
DATE	ENTRIES	REFERENCE	DEBITS	CREDITS
1998				
1 Jan	Cash		$50,000	
	Owner's Investment			$50,000

You already know that whenever the owner of a business invests cash into his or her business, cash is increased and so is the owner's investment (part of owner's equity). A debit was used to increase the Cash account and a credit was used to increase the Owner's Investment account.

In the next transaction, the Bicycle Shoppe buys a building, land, and a truck. Since the Shoppe does not have sufficient cash to pay for all of these assets, it borrows $20,000 and pays the remainder in cash ($23,000). This transaction would be recorded in the general journal as follows:

GENERAL JOURNAL

| | | | AMOUNTS | |
DATE	ENTRIES	REFERENCE	DEBITS	CREDITS
1998				
3 Jan	Land		$10,000	
	Building		$25,000	
	Truck		$8,000	
	Cash			$23,000
	Mortgage			$20,000

Notice in this journal entry that debits were used to increase the assets (Land, Building, and Truck), while credits were used to decrease an asset (Cash), but to increase the liability (Mortgage).

Referring to Lesson 7, where you learned about transactions that affect the income statement, we will now look at how these transactions would affect the general journal.

On January 5, the Shoppe sold two bicycles for a total of $500. As you remember, this transaction caused two changes to the Income Statement. First, it increased the revenue account called Sales by $500, and second, it increased an expense account called Cost of Goods Sold by the cost of these two bicycles, or $200. Remember also that when this transaction caused a change to the Income Statement, it also changed the Balance Sheet in several ways. These bicycles were sold for cash, so the asset cash would increase by $500. The asset inventory would decrease by their cost, or $200 (since they do not belong to the company any longer). The difference between the sale price and the cost ($500 – $200) of $300 would be an increase to retained earnings, which is part of owner's equity.

This transaction would be recorded in the general journal as follows:

GENERAL JOURNAL

			AMOUNTS	
DATE	ENTRIES	REFERENCE	DEBITS	CREDITS
1998				
5 Jan	Cash		$500	
	Sales			$500
	Also:			
5 Jan	Cost of Goods Sold		$200	
	Inventory			$200

Think back to the accounting equation A = L + OE. The sales transaction has increased the left side (assets) by $500, and increased the right side, owner's equity, by the same amount. The second part of this transaction that reduces the inventory also keeps the accounting equation in balance by decreasing owner's equity by $200, and decreases the left side, assets (inventory), by the same amount. In both of these transactions, the debits and the credits are equal.

> **Revenue Accounts** Increased with credits, thus they also increase owner's equity.
>
> **Expense Accounts** Increased with debits, thus they decrease owner's equity.

Looking at another transaction in Lesson 7, "Transactions that Affect the Income Statement," you can see the impact on the general journal. On January 7, Christine's Bicycle Shoppe pays Christine her first week's pay of $100. This transaction would be recorded in the general journal as follows:

GENERAL JOURNAL

| | | | AMOUNTS | |
DATE	ENTRIES	REFERENCE	DEBITS	CREDITS
1998				
7 Jan	Salary Expense		$100	
	Cash			$100

This transaction has decreased the left side of the accounting equation, assets or cash, by $100, and has decreased the right side, owner's equity, with an expense of the same amount. Once again, the debits equal the credits.

Finally, look at one more transaction from Lesson 7, where Christine's Bicycle Shoppe repairs some bicycles for $375. The parts for these repairs cost the company $105, paid for in cash. This transaction is recorded in the general journal as follows:

GENERAL JOURNAL

DATE	ENTRIES	REFERENCE	AMOUNTS DEBITS	CREDITS
1998				
14 Feb	Cash		$375	
	Repairs Revenue			$375
	Also:			
14 Feb	Repairs Expense		$105	
	Cash			$105

Once again, in the first part of this transaction, the left side of the accounting equation is increased by $375, and the right side, owner's equity (via a revenue item), is increased by the same amount.

In the second part of the transaction, the right side is decreased with a credit to an asset (Cash) by $105, and the left side is decreased with a debit to an owner's equity account (Repairs Expense). Thus the equation A = L + OE stays in balance, and the debits equal the credits.

In this lesson you learned how to record business transactions into the original book of entry—the general journal. In Lesson 13 you learn how to "post" these entries to the general ledger and make "adjusting" entries.

POSTING AND ADJUSTING THE ACCOUNTING RECORDS

In this lesson you learn how year-end adjustments are made to a company's records and categorized.

POSTING AND ACCOUNTS

During the month, the journal entries made to record the January transactions would be posted to the general ledger. The *general ledger* is a book containing a record of each account. The Cash account, which probably is the first page (or pages) in the general ledger, may look like this:

CASH				ACCOUNT #101			
DATE	COMMENTS	REF.	DEBIT AMOUNT	DATE	COMMENTS	REF.	CREDIT AMOUNT

Notice that the account has two sides. The left side is used to record the debits and the right side is used to record the credits.

Also notice that the account has a number; in this example, the number is 101. The accounts are usually numbered for a variety of reasons, such as to facilitate referencing, to speed up locating the account in the ledger, and for use instead of the account name. Often the account numbers are divided into five groups—one each for assets (100s), liabilities (200s), owner's equity (300s), revenues (400s), and expenses (500s). This listing of accounts is normally called the *chart of accounts.*

Posting is the process of transferring the information from the general journal to the individual accounts.

After posting the first journal entry (January 1), the Cash account would look like this:

CASH   ACCOUNT #**101**

DATE	COMMENTS	REF.	DEBIT AMOUNT	DATE	COMMENTS	REF.	CREDIT AMOUNT
1 Jan		J-1	$50,000				

The date of the transaction is entered in the date column on the left-hand side. Since the entry was a debit, J-1 is entered in the reference column and that tells you that the journal entry that recorded the transaction can be found on page one of the general journal, and $50,000 is entered in the left-hand amount column.

The other half to this first journal entry (the credit) would be posted to the Owner's Investment account and would look like this:

OWNER'S INVESTMENT   ACCOUNT #301

DATE	COMMENTS	REF.	DEBIT AMOUNT	DATE	COMMENTS	REF.	CREDIT AMOUNT
				1 Jan		J-1	$50,000

Of course, in this instance the data is posted to the right-hand column since the entry is a credit to the account.

Now after posting the first entry, the general journal looks like this:

GENERAL JOURNAL
Page 1

DATE	ENTRIES	REFERENCE	AMOUNTS DEBITS	CREDITS
1998				
1 Jan	Cash	101	$50,000	
	Owner's	301		$50,000
	Equity (To record $50,000 investment by owner)			

You see that the account numbers for the Cash and Owner's Investment accounts have now been entered in the reference column of the journal. This step completes the posting process for the first journal entry. The same procedure is repeated until all journal entries have been posted to the general ledger.

After posting all journal entries recorded in January, the Cash account would look like this:

CASH   ACCOUNT #101

DATE	COMMENTS	REF.	DEBIT AMOUNT	DATE	COMMENTS	REF.	CREDIT AMOUNT
1 Jan	Investment	J-1	$50,000	1 Jan	Assets	J-1	$23,000
3 Jan	Insurance	J-1	$1,500				
5 Jan	Inventory	J-1	$10,000				
6 Jan	Sales	J-1	$500	7 Jan	Salary	J-1	$100
21 Jan	Sales	J-1	$3,500				

If you add the debit and credit sides of the Cash account, you will find that the debits total $54,000 and the credits total $34,600. The difference between these two figures is $19,400. You could say that the Cash account has a debit balance at the end of January. This is the amount reflected on the trial balance for the Cash account (shown below) before adjustments.

TRIAL BALANCE

Typically, accountants prepare a *trial balance* from the general ledger after all transactions have been recorded and posted and prior to determining and recording the adjusting entries. A trial balance is merely a list of all accounts in the general ledger that have a balance other than zero, with the balance in each account shown and the debits and credits totaled. A trial balance of Christine's Bicycle Shoppe on January 31, 1998 would look like this:

CHRISTINE'S BICYCLE SHOPPE
TRIAL BALANCE
JANUARY 31, 1998
(BEFORE ADJUSTING & CLOSING ENTRIES)

	DEBITS	CREDITS
Cash	$19,400	
Accounts Receivable	1,500	
Inventory	10,800	
Prepaid Insurance	1,500	
Land	10,000	
Building	25,000	
Truck	8,000	
Accounts Payable		$3,000
Mortgage Payable (Long-term)		20,000
Owner's Investment		50,000
Retained Earnings	-0-	
Sales		5,500
Repair Revenue	-0-	
Cost of Goods Sold	2,200	
Expenses (Salary)	100	
	$78,500	$78,500

A trial balance is prepared by turning through the pages of the general ledger, locating each account with a balance other than zero, determining what the balance in each account is, and noting the appropriate information on the trial balance. Generally speaking, the trial balance is prepared for two reasons:

- To determine whether the total debits equal the total credits. If they do not equal, some kind of error has been made which must be located and corrected.

- To facilitate the preparation of the adjusting entries which are necessary before the financial statements can be prepared.

You should realize that had Christine's Bicycle Shoppe been in operation prior to this year, a Retained Earnings figure would appear on the present trial balance. The Retained Earnings account will show the beginning retained earnings until the accountant closes the accounts that affect the retained earnings. Lesson 14 discusses closing entries.

ADJUSTING JOURNAL ENTRIES

Accounting records are not kept up to date at all times. To do so would not only be expensive but also would be a waste of time because much of the information is not needed for day-to-day decisions. *Adjusting entries* are steps taken to recognize transactions that have occurred prior to the statements' issuance date, but which have not yet been recorded in the journal.

In the case of Christine's Bicycle Shoppe, there are five items that need to be adjusted: Prepaid Insurance, Building, Truck, interest on the mortgage, and the portion of Accounts Receivable that Christine does not believe the Shoppe will be able to ever collect.

PREPAID INSURANCE

Recall from Lesson 4 that prepaid insurance is listed on the Balance Sheet as an asset. This came about because Christine's Bicycle Shoppe bought insurance in advance of using it. By the end of January (since this was a three-year policy), 1/36th of it had been used or became an expense. To recognize the "using up" of this asset (called Prepaid Insurance on the Balance Sheet), an expense called Insurance Expense is increased by $41.67 ($1,500/36 months). The asset itself is no longer worth the full amount paid, since it now represents only the remaining 35 months. If you think back to the accounting equation again—A = L + OE—the left-hand side of the equation is reduced by $41.67 (Prepaid Insurance), and the right side is also reduced, because of Insurance Expense, by the same amount, $41.67.

BUILDING AND TRUCK

Long-term assets like Building and Truck have a finite life. Their original (historical) cost is therefore spread over their useful lives. This process is called *depreciation*. In order to depreciate these two assets, you need to know the life expectancy of each. In other words, how long will these assets produce income for the business? In our example, you can assume that the building has a life expectancy of 25 years, and the truck has an expectancy of 5 years. To depreciate these two assets, you should divide the historical cost by the life expectancy.

$$\text{Truck} = \frac{\$8,000 \text{ (historical cost)}}{\text{Life Expectancy (5)}} = \$1,600 \text{ (Depreciation per year)}$$

$$\text{Building} = \frac{\$25,000 \text{ (historical cost)}}{\text{Life Expectancy (25)}} = \$1,000 \text{ (Depreciation per year)}$$

Since you are looking for only the depreciation adjustment for these two assets for the month of January, each number would be divided by 12 (months) to arrive at depreciation for one month.

Truck = $\$1,600/12$ = $133.33 per month

Building = $\$1,000/12$ = $33.33 per month

INTEREST EXPENSE

As you remember, Christine's Bicycle Shoppe has to pay interest on the mortgage that it took out on the land and building. The mortgage was for $20,000 for 10 years at 12 percent per year. The total interest per year is $2,400 ($20,000 × 12 percent). Therefore, each month the business owes the mortgage company one-twelfth of the total, or $200 ($2400/12 months). Since the cash is not owed until the end of the year, Christine's Bicycle Shoppe has created another liability called Interest Payable that is due at the end of the year. The amount of this liability is the same as the Interest Expense of $200.

ACCOUNTS RECEIVABLE WRITE-OFFS

At the end of January, Christine concluded that the Shoppe was not going to be able to collect $175 from one of the customers that had promised to pay. In order to recognize this on the financial statements, she created an expense category called Bad Debts Expense. This expense is increased by the amount of the receivable that will not be collected, and the Accounts Receivable account is reduced by the same amount.

Methods of Writing Off Bad Debt   The method that Christine used to write off the bad debt is called the Direct Write-Off Method. It is used by some businesses today. However, the method that is more widely used is called the Allowance Method.

Bad Debt Does Not Affect Cash   You should note that the Shoppe's bad debt expense of $175 reduces the net income in the same way as other expenses that use cash. Even though this one does not use cash, it reduces another asset— accounts receivable.

After the adjusting journal entries are recorded in the journal, they must be posted to the accounts in the general ledger, just like the earlier journal entries. After the adjusting entries are posted, the accountant may prepare another trial balance to help in the preparation of the actual financial statements, or the accountant may be able to prepare the statements by using the general ledger only. A trial balance prepared at this time would look like this:

CHRISTINE'S BICYCLE SHOPPE
TRIAL BALANCE (AFTER ADJUSTMENTS, BEFORE CLOSING)
JANUARY 31, 1998

	DEBITS	CREDITS
Cash	$19,400	
Accounts Receivable	1,325	
Inventory	10,800	
Prepaid Insurance	1,458.33	
Land	10,000	
Building	25,000	
Accumulated Depreciation—Building	(33.33)	
Truck	8,000	
Accumulated Depreciation—Truck	(133.33)	
Accounts Payable		$3,000
Interest Payable		200
Mortgage Payable (Long-term)		20,000
Owner's Investment		50,000
Retained Earnings		-0-
Sales		5,500
Repair Revenue	-0-	
Cost of Goods Sold	2,200	
Salaries Expense	100	
Insurance Expense	41.67	
Depreciation Expense	166.66	
Interest Expense	200	
Bad Debt Expense	175	
	$78,700	$78,700

There are some differences between this trial balance and the one earlier in this lesson, which shows the trial balance before the adjusting journal entries. First, four new accounts have been created: Insurance Expense, Depreciation Expense, Accumulated Depreciation, and Interest Expense.

The account called Insurance Expense represents the amount of the used-up prepaid insurance for one month. It was increased by $41.67 at the same time that Prepaid Insurance (the asset) was decreased by the same amount.

The account Depreciation Expense was created to represent the depreciation on the two long-term assets, Truck and Building. As these long-term assets get older, accountants set up a separate account called a contra-asset instead of reducing the long-term assets directly. For long-term assets, the contra account is called Accumulated Depreciation. Each long-term asset has a separate contra-asset account (Accumulated Depreciation—Truck and Accumulated Depreciation—Building).

But what about land? Land, even though it is a long-term asset, does not depreciate, and it does not have an accumulated depreciation contra-asset account.

The last new account is Interest Expense. This account represents the amount of interest that has been paid (or in some cases is due to be paid, but not yet paid). In our example, this is $200 per month on the mortgage.

In this lesson you learned more about the "bookkeeping process." You learned how to post to the accounting ledgers and how to make adjusting entries. In Lesson 14 you learn how financial statements can be used to evaluate the future short-term success of a business.

USING FINANCIAL STATEMENTS FOR SHORT-TERM ANALYSIS

In this lesson you learn how financial statements can be used to evaluate the future short-term success of a business.

I've divided the subject of how financial statements can be used into two major parts—how they can be used in the near future (this lesson), and how they can be used to evaluate a company's future beyond the near-term (Lesson 15). Near-term is usually defined as one month to one year.

The most important question in deciding a company's near-term future is whether the company will be able to pay its debts when they come due. If not, the firm may be forced into bankruptcy and perhaps forced to cease operations.

> **!** **Profit and Cash Are Not Interchangeable**
> Remember that profits and cash are not the same in the short run. That is, a profitable company can be very short on cash, and an unprofitable firm may have excess cash.

CURRENT AND QUICK RATIOS

To predict whether a company is going to survive in the short-term, you should look first at the Balance Sheet. Compare the company's current assets with its current liabilities (debts that must be paid within 12 months). This ratio of current assets to current liabilities is referred to as the *current ratio*. Also widely used is the comparison of the firm's quick assets to the current liabilities. (*Quick assets* are current assets that can be quickly turned into cash. Usually these assets include cash, current receivables, and marketable securities—in other words, current assets minus inventory and prepaid items.) This ratio of quick assets to current liabilities is referred to as the *quick* (or *acid test*) *ratio*.

Before you can decide whether a firm has sufficient current assets or quick assets to cover its current liabilities, you need to know what the current and quick ratios were in the preceding periods. You also need to know the environmental conditions that existed then as compared to now. It is also useful to know this information about similar companies in the industry.

You can get the average ratios for various industries from publications such as *Moody's, Standard & Poor, Dun & Bradstreet,* and *Robert Morris Associates.*

> **!** **No Substitute for Research** Unfortunately, there is no easy method of obtaining the information about present and past environmental conditions. For this information you must read widely and be sensitive to changing conditions.

The "rules of thumb" used to decide whether the firm has sufficient funds to meet it debts in the near future are 2:1 for the current ratio and 1:1 for the quick ratio. In general, when a firm has twice as many current assets as current liabilities and as many quick assets as current liabilities, it should be able to meet its debts as they come due in the near future. Of course, there are exceptions to this "rule of thumb," depending on the year in question and the particular industry. In general, the larger the current and quick ratios, the greater the probability that a company can pay its debts in the near future.

> **!** **More Isn't Always Better**   These ratios can be too large. A company's profitability is reduced whenever it has too large a proportion of any particular type of asset, including cash.

WORKING CAPITAL

Another important factor in addition to these two ratios is the firm's *working capital*. This is calculated by subtracting the current liabilities from the current assets. This calculation, like the ones shown earlier, must be compared to the past working capital figures for the company. In addition, it is necessary to compare the working capital to the cash flow of the firm, as you calculated in Lesson 8. How much working capital a firm should have depends upon its cash flow. If a business receives and/or disburses an average of $7,000,000 per week, it should have a larger working capital balance than a firm that receives and/or disburses $7,000 per week.

The working capital is a cushion. It allows management to make errors in its estimate of future cash receipts and disbursements and still be able to pay its debts when they fall due. For example, if management estimates both cash receipts and disbursements for the next 30 days to be $30,000, and for some reason receipts total only $25,000 and disbursements total

$35,000, the firm must have either sufficient working capital at the beginning of the month or good credit with its bankers. If this is not the case, the firm will find itself out of business (or the creditors may take control).

> **!** **Cash Flow Affects Working Capital**   The calculation of working capital will not help a great deal unless it is related to the firm's cash flow.

In deciding whether a company is going to survive the near-term, you should also look at the composition of its current assets. That is, you want to see that each of the various current asset items is a desirable size. In this regard, your main interest centers on receivables and inventory items.

Inventories and receivables sometimes may become too large. Receivables may become too large because customers delay their payments or because the company changed its credit policy so that sales are made to people or firms who are greater credit risks or who are slower in paying off their debts. Inventories get too large when, for example, management overestimates the demand for the company's products and either buys or makes too many items. These situations have negative implications for the near-term business prospects.

INVENTORY TURNOVER RATIO

To determine whether inventories are a reasonable size, you can calculate the *inventory turnover ratio* (cost of goods sold divided by average inventory). Average inventory is defined as the beginning inventory balance plus the ending inventory balance divided by 2. This represents the number of times that the inventory "turned over" during a particular period of time. There is no widely used rule of thumb available to gauge inventory turnover ratios. To decide whether the inventory turnover figure for a firm is desirable, you must look at previous turnover figures of the firm, turnover figures of other similar firms, and industry-wide averages. Too high a turnover figure would suggest that sales are being lost due to shortage of inventory; too low a turnover figure may suggest that demand for the goods is falling, that some of the inventory cannot be sold, or that prices must be reduced. Too low a turnover figure may indicate only that as of the Balance Sheet date, too much cash has been invested in inventory items.

AVERAGE COLLECTION PERIOD

To determine whether the balance in accounts receivable is too large (or too small), you can calculate the *average collection period*. Average collection period equals account receivables divided by average sales per day. Average sales per day is equal to annual sales divided by 365 days. You must rely more on the firm's previous average collection period figures in evaluating the result and less on the figures of other firms and industry-wide figures in this case because firms' credit policies and their mix of cash sales and sales on account differ widely. If the average collection period has been increasing, it may indicate increasing difficulty for the firm to collect its receivables as they come due.

Once you decide that the company is going to survive in the near future, then you can turn to estimating its long-term future prospects. But not all financial statement users are interested in the long-term prospects. For example, bankers who have made or contemplate making short-term loans (30-day,

60-day, or even 6-month loans) are mainly concerned with determining whether the borrowing company will be able to repay their loans when they come due.

These statement users will attempt to forecast the company's cash flow for the time period during which their loans are expected to be outstanding. For this reason, the cash flow statement discussed in Lesson 8 becomes very important.

But of those users who are mostly interested in the short-term, like the bankers, some will have an interest in the long-term too. The bankers must be aware of what is happening now and what the future looks like for all of their customers to decide to whom they can loan money and to estimate their own future cash flows.

In this lesson you learned how financial statements can be used to evaluate the short-term success of a business. In Lesson 15 you learn how these financial statements can be used to evaluate a business in the long-term.

USING FINANCIAL STATEMENTS FOR LONG-TERM ANALYSIS

In this lesson you learn how financial statements can be used to evaluate the long-term success of a business.

As you begin to look beyond the short-term success of a company, the main focus of your attention shifts from information presented on the Balance Sheet to information presented on the Income Statement. The approach is to look at the past, attempt to see trends, and project the past performance into the future.

The long-term future of a company depends, to a very large extent, upon the ability of the company's employees. One of your main goals is to determine how well the employees have done in the past and what kind of job are they doing now.

The information that you gathered in Lesson 14 with regard to the near-term future prospect gives you valuable clues to current performance. However, this is not sufficient to draw a reliable conclusion about the long-term prospects of the company. You also need to study this information and compare it to information about other companies, especially with regard to the following:

- Rate of return on investment

- Net profit percentage of sales

- Percentage of various expenses to sales

- Rate of growth of sales

- Earnings per share

- Extraordinary gains and losses

- Price/earnings ratio

- Number of times interest and preferred stock dividends were earned

- Total liabilities to total assets

- Dividend payout ratio

QUALITY OF EARNINGS

In analyzing financial statements, keep in mind the "quality of earnings" of the company being analyzed. The quality of earnings concept is used by both creditors and investors who understand that the bottom line of all organizations is not equal. Companies with higher quality of earnings receive higher credit limits, lower interest costs, and higher stock prices.

WHAT PRODUCES A HIGHER QUALITY OF EARNINGS?

Several factors cause the quality of earnings of one organization to be higher than another's. Some of these factors include:

- Good labor relations
- The majority of net income coming from continuing operations as opposed to one-time transactions
- Quick conversion of sales into cash; in other words, a relatively low average collection period
- An appropriate debt/equity ratio
- A fully funded pension liability
- Stable earning trends
- Highly developed brand loyalty among consumers
- Stable or increasing market share
- An unqualified audit opinion

RATE OF RETURN ON INVESTMENT

The rate of return on investment is probably the most important single financial statistic. It comes as close as any figure can to reflecting how well a company has done.

Return on Investment (ROI) is usually calculated as follows:

Rate of return (ratio) = $\dfrac{\text{Net Income}}{\text{Average Stockholder's Equity}}$

Rate of return (percentage) = $\dfrac{\text{Net Income} \times 100}{\text{Average Stockholder's Equity}}$

Average Stockholder's Equity   (Beginning Stockholder's Equity Balance + Ending Stockholder's Equity Balance) / 2.

> **!** **Equity by Any Other Name** *Stockholder's equity* is the term used in a corporation, whereas *owner's equity* is the term used in a proprietorship and partnership.

Rate of return depicts how much money was earned as a percentage as compared to the amount the owners invested in the business. In the example in Lesson 3, Christine invested $50,000 into the business on January 1. Because the beginning owner's equity was $50,000 on January 1, and the ending owner's equity was $60,385 on December 31, the average was $55,192.50. Since net income for 1998 was $10,385, Christine earned 18.8 percent on her investment ($10,385/$55,192.50).

Look at how well a company did this year as compared to last year by comparing the rate of return figure for each of the two years. You should also compare one company's results to another in the same industry.

> **!** **Compare Apples to Apples** In making these comparisons to prior years' values or to other companies' values, you must be alert as to what estimates were made and which generally accepted accounting principles were used. If the estimates that comprise net income are not the same between years, or between companies, this ratio cannot be compared.

SALES-BASED RATIOS OR PERCENTAGES

To be able to predict future profitability, you need to examine your company's and other companies' past sales and expenses. One such ratio that aids in this analysis is the *net profit percentage of sales* (Net Income / Sales × 100). An increase in this percentage as compared to that of previous years may indicate that the company is operating more efficiently because more sales were made with fewer expenses. Also, when the net profit percentage of sales ratio is higher for one company than another, it may indicate that one company was more efficient than the other.

> **!** **Use Similar Practices** Again, keep in mind that the different companies being compared may have used different GAAP to arrive at their net income calculations.

To help verify these hunches and to gain better insight into operational changes, you should compare a variety of different expenses to the total sales figure. You should calculate ratios like the following:

Cost of goods sold / Sales

Selling and delivery expenses / Sales

General and administrative expenses / Sales

Depreciation expenses / Sales

Lease and rental expenses / Sales

Repairs and maintenance expenses / Sales

Advertising / Sales

Research and development / Sales

Another helpful sales-based ratio is the rate of growth of sales from one *period* to the next. You would find it very informative to learn that Christine's Bicycle Shoppe sales increased 10 percent from one year to the next, and 20 percent over the next two years, and 30 percent over the next two, and so on. The pattern of sales over the most recent years of a company's life can help you form an estimate of expected future sales.

> **!** **Be an Environmentalist** Be aware of the past and present environmental conditions and make educated guesses as to how those conditions will change in the future.

EARNINGS DATA

The *earnings per share* (EPS) figure and the *price/earnings* (P/E) ratio are, along with the rate of return on investment ratio, the most widely used information about business corporations.

> **!** **Corporations Only** Both the P/E ratio and EPS can be calculated only for businesses that have been incorporated.

Earning per share is simply the net income of a business divided by the number of common shares outstanding. To learn the most from this ratio, compare the earnings per share figures of a company over a period of five to ten years, and compare it with those of other companies in the same industry.

When looking at net income for a company, you must also consider the makeup of that number. That is, *extraordinary gains or losses* are often included. These are income/expense items that are not considered to be recurring. Since you want to project the past into the future, you want to eliminate from the past data those gains and losses that are not expected to occur again in the future. Therefore, the EPS figure that you will find most useful is the EPS before extraordinary gains and losses. However, you should also look at the extraordinary items and decide for yourself whether they may occur again in the future.

The price/earnings ratio is calculated by dividing the market price per share of that company's stock by the earnings per share of the company.

$$\text{Price/Earnings Ratio} = \frac{\text{Market Price per Share}}{\text{Earnings per Share}}$$

The price/earnings ratio can give you some very useful ideas about what other people expect of the future of a company. For example, when a company's stock is selling for 50 times its earnings (P/E ratio of 50 to 1) and the average P/E ratio for most stocks in that industry is 15 to 1, you may conclude that the company's earnings are going to increase considerably in the future, or that the price of the stock is going up between now and the time the present buyers will want to sell the stock.

In general, when the P/E ratio of a company's stock is significantly higher than average, the buyers of the stock expect the company to prosper; when the ratio is lower than average, buyers are not optimistic about the company's future.

LONG-TERM DEBT POSITION

Some people believe that a company that borrows money is not as good or as well managed as a company that operates without borrowing. This belief is not necessarily true. Borrowing money often enables a company to increase the net income for the stockholders without increasing their investment.

For example, say that two firms, Company A and Company B, both have assets totaling $100,000, liabilities totaling $10,000, and stockholder's equity totaling $90,000, and they both expect a net income next year of $9,000. This represents a return of 10 percent.

Return on Stockholder's Equity Net Income / Average Stockholder's Equity, or $9,000/ $90,000 =10%.

Now assume that management is considering the purchase of $40,000 worth of assets. These assets will produce additional annual net income before interest expense of $4,000. The companies have two choices. They can borrow the $40,000 at 6 percent interest, or they can have the investors put the additional $40,000 into the businesses.

If Company A borrows the $40,000, its net income next year would be $10,600 ($9,000 + $4,000 – $2,400) before income taxes. The $2,400 reduction to net income is the interest on the loan ($40,000 × 6 percent). Thus, the rate of return on stockholder's equity would be 11.7 percent ($10,600 / $90,000 = 11.7 percent).

Company B did not borrow the $40,000. Instead, the owners invested this money. Net income would still increase by $4,000 to $13,000 ($9,000 + $4,000). There would be no interest expense, and the return on stockholder's equity would be $13,000 / $130,000 (the original $90,000 + the additional $40,000). Thus, in the situation with Company B not borrowing the additional $40,000, its rate of return on stockholder's equity is 10 percent. Company A did borrow the additional $40,000, and thus ended up with a return on stockholder's equity of 11.7 percent.

> **!** **Risky Business**   Too much debt can make a company too "risky." During periods of downturns in the economy, it may not be able to repay its debt.

One way to determine if a company has put itself into a risky position is to calculate the number of times interest was earned and the ratio of total liabilities to total assets.

To calculate the number of times that interest was earned, divide the interest expense into the net income before interest expense and before income taxes. You use the income figure before income taxes because interest expense is deductible for income tax purposes.

$$\text{Number of Times Interest Is Earned} = \frac{\text{Net Income Before Interest and Taxes}}{\text{Interest Expense}}$$

The larger this ratio, the easier it is for the company to meet its interest payments, and the less likely the company would go out of business.

To calculate the ratio of total liabilities to total assets, divide total liabilities by total assets. The idea here is that the larger the ratio, the more risky the company.

> **!** **No Promises** Of course, a company with a large liability to asset ratio may prosper while a company without any debt at all may fail. The liability to asset ratio, like any ratio, gives you only a part of the total picture.

DIVIDEND DATA

Additional information about a company can be obtained by looking at the cash dividends that it has paid over the past several years. You would, for instance, calculate the dividend payout ratio, which is total cash dividends declared during the year divided by the net income of the year.

$$\text{Dividend Payout Ratio} = \frac{\text{Dividends Declared}}{\text{Net Income}}$$

If the ratio is large, the company is paying a large portion of the funds earned to the stockholders and not reinvesting them in the company. If this ratio is small or if the company pays no dividends whatsoever, the company may be growing rapidly and using the funds to finance this growth.

FOOTNOTES

Almost all financial statements of companies larger than the small business have footnotes attached to them. In any case, the footnotes are as important as the fine print in a contract.

When you examine a company's annual report, consider reading the footnotes first, then examine the statements and then read the president's message and the rest of the "advertising" last.

The footnotes contain a wide variety of information. Examples include: terms of pension plans, terms of stock options outstanding, nature and expected outcome of any pending lawsuits, terms of a long-term lease agreement, and probable effects of forced sale of properties in a foreign country. It should be apparent that the footnotes provide many clues about a company's future.

CONCLUSION

Analyzing financial statements is very useful to many users. Without the use of historical data, no predictions could be made about the future of a company. The more you read financial statements, use them, and work with them, the better your decisions about the future of your company and those you wish to invest in will become.

In this lesson you learned how financial statements can be used to evaluate the long-term success of a business. In Lesson 16 you learn how to prepare and use a budget in your business and personal life.

Using a Budget in Your Business and Professional Life

In this lesson you learn what a budget is, how to prepare one, and how it can be useful to you in your business and professional life.

What Is a Budget?

The *budget* is a detailed plan that outlines future expectations in quantitative terms. Budgeting is an important part of our society. Budgets can be used for various reasons. You can budget your time, you can use a budget to plan and control your future income and expenses, businesses can use budgets for planning for future capital expenditures, and governmental agencies can use budgets of revenues and expenses in order to determine their future tax needs.

Planning vs. Control

These two terms are often confused, when in fact they are two distinct concepts. *Planning* is the development of future objectives *and* the preparation of budgets to meet these objectives.

Control, on the other hand, involves ensuring that the objectives established during the planning phase are attained. A good budgeting system takes into consideration both the plan and the control.

ADVANTAGES OF BUDGETING

Whether the budget is for personal use or that of your business, the major advantage of using a budget is that it gives formality to the planning process. If the budget involves other people, it also communicates the plan to these other people. Once the budget has been established, it serves as a benchmark for evaluating the actual results. One of the major processes within an organization is to coordinate and integrate the plans and the goals of the various departments.

With the advent of personal computers and spreadsheet programs, budgeting has been simplified. The computers can maintain and implement the budgets at a small cost. In addition, it becomes easy to make changes on a regular basis to view "what if" situations that come up, thus allowing the individual or the manager the ability to more easily make decisions based on these anticipated results.

The success or failure of budgets within an organization is usually enhanced by the participation of the managers. The managers feel as if they are part of the "team" and are usually more apt to fulfill the goals that they have had a direct role in developing. This doesn't mean that these budgets should not be subject to review by higher management; however, any changes should be made with the involvement of the original individuals.

THE MASTER BUDGET

The master budget is a network of many separate budgets that are interdependent. An example of this network is exhibited in Figure 16.1.

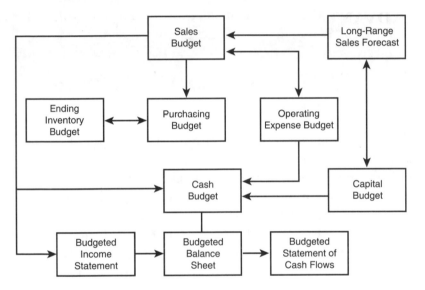

Figure 16.1   A master budget includes many separate but interdependent budgets.

SALES BUDGET

Let's assume that Christine's Bicycle Shoppe wants to prepare a budget for the month of March, 1998. As indicated by Figure 16.1, the first thing that the business should do is estimate the sales revenue for the upcoming month. This budget is prepared by multiplying the expected unit sales for each product by its anticipated unit selling price. Assume that in this case that total will be $45,000.

In addition to the normal sales of bicycles, Christine's Bicycle Shoppe has been increasing its revenue from repairs. During the month of March, 1998, the revenue from repairs will be budgeted at $950.

COST OF GOODS SOLD AND ENDING INVENTORY

Further assume that the ending inventory at the end of February, 1998 is $9,000. On average, the shop has a 60 percent profit margin (remember that *profit margin*, or *gross profit*, equals the sales minus cost of goods sold). Since sales are budgeted to be $45,000, the gross profit would be $27,000 (sales of $45,000 – cost of goods sold of $18,000). Further assume that since the company is growing, the Bicycle Shoppe determines that it wants ending inventory to grow from the previous months in anticipation of growing sales in the future. It has budgeted ending inventory for March, 1998 to be $12,000.

Purchases is calculated by the following formula:

Beginning Inventory

+ Purchases

– Ending Inventory

Cost of Goods Sold

In this example:

Beginning Inventory (February's Ending Inventory)	$9,000
+ Purchases	????
− Ending Inventory	12,000
Cost of Good Sold	$18,000

By working backwards, it is calculated that purchases for the month of March must be $21,000.

OPERATING EXPENSES

The next items to be budgeted are the operating expenses. During the month of February, these expenses were $7,565, or approximately 21 percent of sales for that month. Again, assuming that this percentage remains fairly constant, and that during the month of March sales are budgeted to be $45,000, operating expenses would be budgeted at $9,450 (21 percent of $45,000).

CAPITAL BUDGET

To determine if any additional space would need to be rented or built, the business must next do a long-range sales forecast. Assuming that the business is growing at a fairly constant rate, the Bicycle Shoppe budgets that within two years, another building must be purchased. Christine anticipates that the cost of this building with sufficient space for the next five years after completion would be $48,000. Therefore, the capital budget per month for the next two years (that is, when the purchase will have to be actually made, and Christine does not want any additional debt on this building) would be $2,000.

With this information, it is now possible to create a cash budget and a budgeted income statement, balance sheet, and cash flow. Let's examine this information.

BUDGETED INCOME STATEMENT

The budgeted income statement would look like this:

CHRISTINE'S BICYCLE SHOPPE
BUDGETED INCOME STATEMENT
FOR THE PERIOD ENDED MARCH, 1998

Sales	$45,000
Cost of Goods Sold	18,000
Gross Profit	$27,000
Operating Expenses	9,450
Net Income from Operations	$17,550
Other Revenue:	
Repair Revenue	950
Net Income	$18,500

THE CASH BUDGET

In order to calculate the budgeted ending cash balance for March, 1998, you need to know the beginning cash balance. This figure is the same as the ending cash balance in February. Assume that this number is $15,000. A number of other assumptions need to be made as well. With sales being predicted for the month of March at $45,000 plus $950 for repairs, you need to know how much of these sales will be in cash and how much will be on accounts receivable. In this example let's assume 75 percent of both the bicycle sales and repair work will be for cash. Thus the cash receipts for March from March sales will be $34,462.50 ($45,950 × 75 percent).

Assuming that this same ratio applies to the preceding month (that is, 75 percent of the sales were for cash, and the other 25 percent were on account), then the 25 percent that was sold on account in February will be collected in March. (This is making the assumption that there were no bad debts.) Again, with the assumption that the sales and the repair work for February totaled $38,500, the cash to be collected in March on these February sales would be $9,625 ($38,500 × 25 percent).

These same assumptions have to be made with the $21,000 of purchases for March and the $17,500 for February. Thus, the amount of cash expended in March would be the cash purchases for March purchases of $15,750 ($21,000 × 75 percent) + $4,375, the payment of the account payables due in March from February purchases ($17,500 × 25 percent).

Continuing with the assumption that part of expenditures each month are made for cash and part on account, make the assumption that with the operating expenses, 80 percent are made for cash in the month of use and 20 percent are made on account. Thus, in March, the operating expenses were $9,450 and assume that in February the operating expenses were $8,500. Using the same logic as we just did with the purchases, the total cash outlay for operating expenses in March would be $9,260 ($9,450 × 80 percent + $8,500 × 20 percent).

The last cash "expenditure" that Christine's Bicycle Shoppe made during the month of March is the $2,000 that the business "put aside" for the future purchase of a building. This cash transaction is neither an expenditure nor a reduction in cash. It is simply going from one bank account to another to be set aside for the future purchase of a building. The only reason for the transaction at all is to make sure that the cash left in the operating cash account is not "accidentally" spent prior to the purchase of the building.

It is now possible to calculate the ending cash balance:

CHRISTINE'S BICYCLE SHOPPE
BUDGETED ENDING CASH BALANCE
FOR THE PERIOD ENDED MARCH, 1998

Beginning Cash	$15,000
Add:	
Cash Receipts from March Sales	34,462
Cash Receipts from February Sales	9,625
Subtract:	
Cash Purchases for March	15,750
Cash Payments on Accounts Payable for February	4,375
Cash Payments for Operating Expenses in March	7,560
Cash Payments for Operating Expenses in February	1,700
Ending Cash Balance	$29,702

The example presented here is for a business such as Christine's Bicycle Shoppe. However, the same concepts can be applied to preparing a personal budget and the same benefits will be derived.

In this lesson you learned the meaning of a budget, the value of preparing one, and the ways in which the components interrelate. In Lesson 17 you learn how accountants can best use the Internet and the World Wide Web.

INTERNET FOR ACCOUNTANTS

In this lesson you learn how to access the Internet and the World Wide Web (WWW) and what online resources are available in the field of accounting.

WHAT IS THE INTERNET?

The Internet is a catch-all term used to describe a large network of computers throughout the world that have the capability to communicate with each other. It has been called a global information system.

The word *Internet* literally means a *network of networks*. Probably the best definition of the Internet (or "Net") has come from an anonymous author who has called the Internet a herd of performing elephants with diarrhea—massive, difficult to redirect, awe-inspiring, entertaining, and a source of mind-boggling amounts of excrement when we least expect it.

WHAT IS THE WORLD WIDE WEB?

Different from the Internet, which refers to the physical side of this information system, the World Wide Web refers to a body of knowledge that is shared on the Internet. "The Web," as it is called, has been thought of for years as a universal database that links similar pieces of information so that the user can easily find them. The official description describes the World Wide Web as a "wide-area hypermedia information retrieval initiative aiming to give universal access to a large universe of documents."

Every location of every page on the Web has an address. This address allows users who know this address to go directly to the site. (The author's address is *http://www.nevada.edu/~label*.) If you do not know this address you usually are able to find it through the search process described later in this chapter. Most addresses begin with *http://* and continue with additional information about the particular location. Often the letters *www*, which indicate the World Wide Web, follow directly after the *http://*.

WHAT DO YOU NEED TO COMMUNICATE ON THE NET?

The equipment that is needed to log on to the Internet consists of a computer, a modem, and a link to a server. With them you can be part of this massive system. Millions of people are connected to the Net, and it is estimated that an additional 200,000 individuals and companies are connected every month.

One interesting thing about the Internet is that your type or size of computer becomes anonymous once you're connected. In other words, the system does not tell the difference between a Macintosh and an IBM. The only factors that make a difference are the amount of memory that your computer has and the speed of your modem. Large amounts of memory and a fast modem give you faster access to the information available on the Net.

You can achieve access to the Net in several ways. Many companies' computers are directly linked to the Internet, and employees and contractors of those companies are often able to get a "link" into the system. From your home, you can become a member of a company that provides e-mail and Internet access. Some of these companies include America Online, CompuServe, and Prodigy. In addition to these national companies, most major cities throughout the world have companies that will provide a link through your modem to the Internet. Almost all of these companies charge a flat monthly fee for unlimited (or nearly unlimited) usage.

WHAT CAN YOU USE THE INTERNET FOR?

The information that you can access is limited only by your imagination. You can use the Internet to send electronic mail (e-mail) to anyone in the world who is connected. You can retrieve information, gain access to bulletin boards where subject matters vary from hobbies to technical jargon and—don't tell the boss—you can play games. In addition to sending e-mail to friends, colleagues, and family around the world, once on the Web you can do such things as get information about the law, or even write a letter to your congressman or the president of the United States. You can study history, find the weather in any part of the world for today or tomorrow, make an airline or hotel reservation, or get information about your favorite professional or college sports team, including the score of a game being played right now. The list goes on!

How Can You Search for Information on the Web?

One of the early challenges of the Internet was that there was (and is) a large amount of information floating around out there but not a very easy way to locate specific interests. As time went on companies developed what have become known as "search engines." These services allow the user to narrow his or her search to a topic or a word. The engine then provides links to addresses dealing with that particular topic.

The following list contains several of the "search engines" available today. However, you should keep in mind that none of them is all inclusive, and often when searching for information on a topic, the use of two or more of these sites listed below is helpful and often necessary.

- Alta Vista—*http://altavista.digital.com/*
- Excite—*http://www.excite.com/*
- Infoseek Guide—*http://guide.infoseek.com/*
- Lycos—*http://www.lycos.com/*
- WebCrawler—*http://webcrawler.com/WebCrawler/WebQuery.html*
- Yahoo!—*http://www.yahoo.com/*

What Resources Are Available for Accountants?

The amount of information for not only accountants but for any professional continues to grow each day. The user can find additional information to that listed below by doing searches for topics of specific interest using one of the search engines described earlier.

The following list is only partial and does not cover all topics of interest to accountants. However, part of the fun of being on the Net is to "surf the Web" to find the links that are most interesting to you and to your particular interests.

- The IRS Home Page

  http://www.irs.ustreas.gov/prod/cover.html

- Accounting Bibliography Search

  http://anet.scu.edu.au/wwwbib/anetbib-search.html

- Accounting Resources on the Web

  http://www.rutgers.edu/Accounting/raw/Internet/Internet.html

- Corporate SEC Filings

  http://www.uni.edu/schmidt/bookmark/html

- Fifty of the Most Overlooked Tax Savings

  http:/infi.net/~jhewitt/taxsave.html

- Job Searches

  http://www.aocnet.com/aoc/qsearch2.qry?fn=begin

- Government Agencies

  http://www.rutgers.edu/Accounting/raw/Internet/govt.htm

- Two Fun Guys and An Accountant (Joke Page)

  http://www.execpc.com/~thorsten/MATERIAL.HTML

- Information on Setting Up a Small Business

  http://www.bcscpa.com/startup.htm

- Investing Resources

  Charles Schwab—*http://www.schwab.com*

  Mutual Funds Home Page—*http://www.channel1.com/ user/fund/index.html*

  etrade—*http://www.etrade.com*

- Stock Quotes

  http://investor.msn.com/home.asp

  http://www.stock.smart.com

  http://www.stae.ct.us/ott/stock.htm

  http://www.webpage.com/hindu/quotes.htm (International)

  http://www.nasdaq.com/

- Newspapers

  New York Times—http://www.nytimes.com

  Wall Street Journal—http://update.wsj.com

You can also find links to newspapers throughout the world on many of the search engines.

Once again, this is just a starter. Have fun "surfing the Net."

In this lesson you learned the basic principles of the Internet and the World Wide Web. You also learned about some of the resources that are available for accountants.

GLOSSARY OF TERMS

Accounting   The process of recording, classifying, and summarizing economic events in a process that leads to the preparation of financial statements.

Accounting Equation   A = L + OE, the formula that depicts the relationships of the various elements of the Balance Sheet—assets, liabilities, and owner's equity.

Accounts Receivable   A promise to pay the company for merchandise or services already received.

Accounts Receivable Write-offs   The process of removing from the books an account receivable that is never going to be paid. These accounts are written off to an expense account.

Accrual Basis of Accounting (also **Accrual Concept)**   The process of recognizing, in the financial statements, revenue when it is earned and expenses as they are incurred regardless of when the cash changes hands.

Adjusting Journal Entries   Steps taken to recognize transactions that have occurred prior to the statement's issue date, but which have not yet been recorded in the journal.

Adverse Audit Report   A report issued by a CPA that concludes that the financial statements are not in accordance with Generally Accepted Accounting Principles (GAAP).

AICPA   American Institute of Certified Public Accountants.

Assets   Valuable resources owned by a business.

Audit   The accumulation and evaluation of evidence about a company's financial statements to determine if they are in accordance with Generally Accepted Accounting Principles (GAAP).

Auditor   An individual who checks the accuracy and fairness of the accounting records of a company and determines if they are in accordance with GAAP.

Authorized Shares   The number of shares a corporation is authorized to sell per their charter from the state in which they incorporated.

Average Collection Period   Accounts receivable / 365.

Balance Sheet   A listing of the assets (items owned), liabilities (items owed), and owner's equity (what belongs to the owner(s)).

"Big Six" Accounting Firms   The largest CPA firms with offices worldwide.

Bottom Line   Net Income.

Budget   A detailed plan that outlines future expectations in quantitative terms.

Capital Budget   The budget for long-term assets.

Capital Stock   Ownership shares in a corporation. There are two types—common stock and preferred stock.

Cash Equivalents   Liquid short-term investments that can quickly be converted into cash.

Certificate in Management Accounting Examination (CMA)   A test prepared and offered by the Institute of Management Accountants designed to test proficiency in management accounting, including periodic reporting and decision analysis.

Certified Public Accountants (CPAs)   Auditors who serve the needs of the general public. Their work includes auditing, tax planning, and preparation and management consulting.

Chart of Accounts   A listing of account numbers for each of the accounts. These numbers are usually divided into five groups: assets, liabilities, owner's equity, revenues, and expenses.

Closing Journal Entries   The journal entries necessary to close the Revenue and Expense Accounts into Retained Earnings.

Common Stock   One type of capital stock issued by a corporation. Common stockholders normally have voting rights.

Compliance Audit   An audit that makes sure the accounting is in compliance with the rules being reviewed.

Conservatism   Choosing the lower or more conservative figures when two or more methods are suitable for presentation on the financial statements.

Consistency   Practices and methods of presentation should be the same year to year and process to process.

Control   Involves ensuring that the objectives established during the planning phase are attained.

Corporation   An "artificial being" independent from its owners. It is a separate legal entity. Corporations can be set up as for-profit or not-for-profit.

Cost of Goods Sold   The historical cost to acquire the merchandise represented in sales.

CPA Examination   A nationally prepared examination necessary for entrance into the public accounting profession.

Credit   The right side of the amount column in a journal or ledger.

Creditors   Those individuals or companies to which money or other assets are owed.

Cumulative Preferred Stock   When the preferred shareholders are not paid a full dividend in any year, then subsequent years' dividend payments to them must be sufficient to cover the previously inadequate dividend payments before any dividends can be paid to the common stockholders.

Debit   The left side of the amount column in a journal or ledger.

Depreciation   The process of allocating the historical cost of a long-term asset over its useful life.

Disclaimer Audit Report   A report issued by an auditor when he or she does not have enough information to determine whether the financial statements are or are not in accordance with the accounting rules.

Dividend Payout Ratio   Dividends Declared / Net Income.

Dividends   A distribution of earnings to stockholders.

Earnings Per Share   Net Income / Number of Common Shares Outstanding.

Entity Concept   The transactions of each business or person are kept separate from those of other organizations or individuals.

Equity   See **Owner's Equity**.

Expenditure   The spending of cash. All expenses are expenditures; however, all expenditures are not expenses. Expenditures that have future benefits are classified as assets.

Expenses   Expenditures that immediately generate revenue.

Extraordinary Gains and Losses   Income or expense items that are not considered to be recurring.

Federal Bureau of Investigation (FBI)   The primary investigative arm of the United States Department of Justice.

Financial Accounting Standards Board (FASB)
Responsible for issuing accounting rules in the United States.

Financial Statements   Reports prepared by companies on the financial status of their businesses.

Financing Activities   Represents the cash that has come into the company or out of the company for the purpose of financing all of the other activities.

General Accounting Office (GAO)   Reports directly to Congress and is charged with examining federal departments and agencies. It is headed by the Comptroller General.

General Journal   The book of original entry where transactions are entered and accumulated.

General Ledger   A book containing a record (or listing) of each account.

Generally Accepted Accounting Principles (GAAP)
A set of rules that govern the preparation of financial statements.

Going Concern Concept   The assumption that a business will continue to operate into the indefinite future.

Governmental Auditor   Individuals who perform the audit function for a governmental organizations.

Gross Profit   The difference between revenue and cost of goods sold.

Historical Cost   The amount that was paid for an item or the amount originally incurred for a debt.

Income Statement   A listing of all revenues and expenses of the business during a specified time period.

Intangible Assets   Those assets that are of value to a business but do not have tangible qualities, but meet all other tests of being an asset.

Internal Auditor   Employed by a company to audit the records of that company. In general, his or her work includes compliance audits and operational audits.

Internal Revenue Service (IRS)   Charged with the collection of federal taxes in the United States.

Internet   A large network of computers throughout the world that have the ability to communicate with each other.

Inventory   An asset held by a business for the purpose of resale.

Inventory Turnover Ratio   Cost of Goods Sold / Average Inventory.

Investing Activities   Purchases of property, plant, or equipment.

Journal   See **General Journal**.

Journal Entries   The entries in the general journal to record transactions.

Liabilities   Obligations to pay others for resources that were furnished to the business.

Long-Term Assets   Those assets that will be converted to cash after a period of one year or more.

Long-Term Liabilities   Those liabilities that will remain as debt to the entity for longer than one year.

Master Budget   A network of many separate budgets that are interdependent.

Materiality   An item is material when its inclusion or exclusion would change a decision of a statement user.

Net Income   Revenue minus expenses.

Net Profit Percentage of Sales   Net Income / Sales × 100.

Number of Times Interest was Earned   Net Income Before Taxes / Interest Expense.

Obtainable Information   Information must be worth more than it costs to obtain and must be obtainable on a timely basis.

Operating Activities   Cash generated from the day-to-day operations of the business.

Operational Audit   A review of an organization's operating procedures for efficiency and effectiveness.

Owner's Equity   The difference between what is owned and what is owed. This residual belongs to the owners.

Par Value   The value attributed to capital stock by the secretary of state of incorporation. In many states, the par value multiplied by the number of shares issued is equal to the legal capital of a corporation.

Participating Preferred Stock   After the preferred stockholders receive their specified dividends, they then participate in excess dividends with the common stockholders.

Partnership   A business entity with one or more owners. The accounting for partnerships is similar to that for proprietorships.

Planning   The development of future objectives and the preparation of budgets to meet these objectives.

Posting   The process of transferring the information in the general journal to the individual accounts.

Preferred Stock   One type of capital stock issued by a corporation. This type of stock is usually preferred in dividends and liquidation.

Price/Earnings (P/E) Ratio   Market Price Per Share / Earnings Per Share.

Proprietorship   A business with one owner.

Qualified Audit Report   A report issued by an auditor when he or she concludes that the financial statements are presented in accordance with GAAP, except for some specified items being different.

Quantifiable Information   Information is easier to understand and use if it is quantified. When it cannot be quantified, it will be shown in the financial statements in narrative form in the footnotes.

Quick Ratio (or Acid Test Ratio)   Quick Assets / Current Liabilities.

Rate of Growth of Sales   Percentage change in sales between two or more years.

Rate of Return on Investment   Net Income / Average Stockholders' Equity.

Realizable Value   Assets should never be shown on the Balance Sheet at more than their realizable value to the firm.

Recognition Principle   Revenue is recognized at the point of the transfer of merchandise or service, not at the point of receiving cash. Expenses are recognized when incurred.

Relevant Information   Information that helps financial statement users to estimate the value of a firm and/or evaluate the firm's management.

Reliable Information   There should be sufficient and objective evidence available to indicate that the information presented is valid.

Retained Earnings   Represents the amount of profit earned by the business since its inception less any money that is taken out or distributed to the owner(s).

Revenue (also **Sales**)   The total amount obtained by an organization for the sale of merchandise or other commodities or from the rendering of services to its customers.

Search Engines   Addresses on the World Wide Web where you can search for topics you are researching.

Securities and Exchange Commission (SEC)   Created by Congress in 1934. The Commission has the legal power to prescribe accounting principles and/or practices that must be followed by companies that fall within its jurisdiction.

Separate Entities   See **Entity Concept**.

Short-Term Assets   Those items that will be converted to cash within one year or less.

Short-Term Liabilities   Those items that will be paid within one year or less.

Stable Monetary Unit Concept   Even though the value of the dollar changes over time (due to inflation), the values that appear on the financial statements are presented at historical cost.

Statement of Cash Flows   One of the four required financial statements. It shows where cash came from and how it was spent during the period of reporting.

Stock Dividends   The distribution of earnings to the stockholders in the form of stock rather than cash.

Stock Splits   An increase in the number of shares outstanding, which causes a decrease in the stock's par value.

Treasury Stock   When a company buys back its own stock and does not cancel it or resell it.

Trial Balance   A list of all accounts in the general ledger that have a balance other than zero.

Understandable Information   Financial information must be comparable.

Unqualified Audit Report   A report issued by an auditor when the financial statements are in accordance with GAAP.

Verifiable Information   Information on the financial statements must be based on sufficient evidence, which leads the user to believe that the resulting statements provide a reliable basis for evaluating the firm and its management.

Working Capital   Current Assets minus Current Liabilities.

World Wide Web (also **Web** or **WWW**)   A universal database that links similar pieces of information on the Internet.

INDEX